The Print in Blueprint

JOYCE SCHLANGER and LAURIE NOBLE

Illustrations by Eric Noble & Joyce Schlanger

Published in the United States in 2014 by Raburn Publishing, a division of Stephen Raburn + Associates, LLC and ThinkBox Press

No part of this publication may be reproduced or distributed in any form or by any means without prior written permission of the publisher.

Visit our website at www.RaburnPublishing.com

ISBN-13: 978-0692341643
ISBN-10: 0692341641

Raburn Publishing loves trees. We use the print-on-demand publishing method to avoid wasting the planet's resources. We also love children. A portion of the proceeds from the sale of our books is donated to worthy children's charities. Thank you for your purchase and supporting the needs of children.

DEDICATION

This book was only possible
With the love and encouragement of family.
So we'd like to say Thank You to:
John, Eric, Bob, Jordan, Taylor, Nate, and Sammie.

With the support that you've provided,
We were able to find the time
To create a vision called Gritty Lasagna
And help awaken the human mind.

So thank you for your sacrifices
And your willingness to be a part
Of something we believe is truly special
And is sure to affect your heart.

...And, of course none of this could have been conceivable without our strong
gritty Italian mothers,
Terry Marziotto Spisak
&
Joyce Lombardi Stevenson
who are two of the "grittiest" individuals we know.

CONTENTS

Preface		vii
Gritty Lasagna		ix
Introduction		xi
Chapter 1	Success	1
Chapter 2	The Nexus Model	13
Chapter 3	Self Awareness	19
Chapter 4	Social Awareness	39
Chapter 5	Emotional Intelligence	53
Chapter 6	Stress	67
Chapter 7	Communication	79
Chapter 8	Choice	95
Chapter 9	Life Plan	113
Chapter 10	Making Footprints	125
Bibliography		127

PREFACE

About The Authors

Laurie Noble and Joyce Schlanger met in 1995 in Charlotte, NC when both worked in the social services field. They immediately clicked and soon realized that they had many parallels in their lives. Both were graduates of West Virginia University and in love with men from Pittsburgh, PA, who they are still happily married to after all these years.

Over time, one thing became very clear; they shared a philosophy regarding human behavior and life. Joyce and Laurie believe that, individually, we hold the key to our own personal happiness and success. Individuals are powerful, not powerless, and we direct our lives by the choices we make. They appreciate the importance of recognizing this power and understand the importance of never giving our individual power away.

One day they were talking and brainstorming some training ideas. Several key concepts kept coming up in the conversation and they realized that there were on to something big. They identified the key to achieving long-term success, and before they knew it, the Gritty Lasagna Philosophy was born.

When Joyce approached me about ideas swirling around in her head about a book, this is the way she described the concept: Gritty Lasagna is about building individual grit, passion and perseverance, to achieve long-term success and to realize one's life dream through the progress of knowledge... to raise individual growth and diminish personal obstacles that impede an individual's ability to attain success. It is this passion and perseverance sustained over a long period of time that empowers us to go after our goals today, tomorrow and far into the future, even when the results we're after aren't immediately realized.

I was intrigued. And once I got a better understanding of the model and became clear that Gritty Lasagna wasn't some strange backwoods Italian fusion recipe, I was on board.

Gritty Lasagna is about recognizing the power we each have to create the life we want and the ability to experience the success we desire by choosing to make changes to those hindrances that stand in our way.

Gritty Lasagna is an inspirational, interactive and instructive guide to unleashing your inner power and achieving your goals - both in the workplace and at home. Written by two awesome and empowered women who use the concepts and messages in Gritty Lasagna in their own daily lives and to inspire and motivate audiences in classrooms and conferences across the country. Gritty Lasagna is more of a movement than a book. It has the potential to change lives.

Once you take a little nibble of Gritty Lasagna, I'm sure you'll dive in for the full course. Keep a copy on your nightstand and coffee table. Sample often.

Stephen Raburn, Publisher

GRITTY LASAGNA

GRITTY LASAGNA, REALLY?!?!?
HOW DID YOU COME UP WITH THAT NAME?

We have had MANY people say, "I love the name. How did you come up with it?" It's a long story and I usually just credit Laurie for her great ability to create analogies and titles with deep meanings for just about anything. As we were writing this book, we had no plans to tell the tale of the Gritty Lasagna name, but when we sent in our final draft to our publisher, he too, yearned for more of an explanation on the Gritty Lasagna name. Apparently there was a feeling of folks being robbed of knowing its true meaning. We were not trying to hide the story; we just did not realize it was publish worthy. Once it was brought to our attention that the name Gritty Lasagna longed to be explained, this quick chapter was added to help provide some clarification. In the process of writing this chapter, it anchored our belief deeper into this philosophy, and secured our belief that Gritty Lasagna is truly something special, and we hope by the time you are done reading this book, it will be special to you, too.

After we developed the model and started writing this book, we could not decide on a name for either one. We threw many clinical names around, but we quickly realized that this is really not who we are. Although we both have clinical backgrounds and respect the need for clinical approaches and research, our style to human behavior modification comes with a lighter, fun, and more approachable place. Clinical is not us…a bit quirky is more of who we are. About this time author David Sedaris had a new book published called *Let's Explore Diabetes with Owls*. The title of his book had absolutely nothing to do with the content that lay inside the pages, but it made you stop and wonder what the book was actually about. We both felt it. We connected with this bit of quirky and whimsy. We connected with having a title that made people ask, "What is this book about?" For months we racked our brains and spent hours brainstorming quirky, funny, interesting, titles, but nothing stuck. We wanted an interesting name, but we felt a need to have meaning behind which title we chose, even if it only had meaning to us. I was tired of calling the book, "the book" and the model, "the model." I needed it to have some identity, so we started to call the book, Penelope, and the model, Oscar. Don't ask me why. I have no clue. They were just names that I threw out and they stuck. The book and model had a name at least for the time being.

The names Penelope and Oscar served their purpose. It was one less thing we had to focus on when we first started writing the book, and we knew the real titles would come to us in time. One day Laurie texted me, and said, "what about Gritty Lasagna?" I have to be honest; when she sent this name to me I was not feeling it at all. I had this belief that when I heard the title, I would immediately feel it in my gut. OK, I was not feeling it, but if I have learned anything in life, it has been not to close my mind to other possibilities, so I mulled it over. I understood the Gritty part of the name since the model was about building grit, but Lasagna? What did lasagna have to do with anything? It did not make sense to me, but I knew Laurie had made a connection that had meaning to the word lasagna, even if I could not see it. I needed her to explain. I contacted her and in seconds, I knew she was definitely feeling it. She explained that she started thinking about the fact that we were both Italian and the thought of lasagna popped into her head. She talked about how lasagna is a layering process just like our model, and explained that at the core all lasagna is the same. We may put different ingredients into our recipe but in the end it all makes lasagna. This correlated with our thought that individuals using our Nexus Model will focus on different components of the model at different degrees, but in the end we are all working toward being grittier to reach our desired goals and life dream. As Laurie and her husband Eric explained their complete vision regarding this title, I was won over. Gritty Lasagna was it. The name Gritty Lasagna was not just a title. It was bigger than that. It was a philosophy and a brand. It represented so much more than just this one book. It represents our training company, our ideas for a series of books, and our vision that encompasses everything we have ever imagined by signifying that each layer of our vision can be part of a one grand plan. Gritty Lasagna represents our need to be grittier to achieve each layer in our business dream, and it represents both our differences and similarities that all have a place in our path to success. It embraces our past, as well as, offers a path to a future we want to attain. For us all, it provides a way to harness the power we have, and paves a path of stepping-stones that are achievable and useful, creating a viable approach to positive change and ultimate accomplishment.

Laurie and I are a great team. We trust each other and respect the strengths that we both bring to the table. We complement each other well, and provide balance to the process. If I had not trusted Laurie that day she called me and respected her process, I could have easily blown off the name Gritty Lasagna, and this particular path would not have been chosen. I was able to put my ego aside and recognize that I do not have the answers for everything, and sometimes when you put your faith in others, grand things occur. We are asking you to put your faith in us and in our Nexus Model. We are asking you to believe in yourself, in your dream and in your ability to succeed. Allow the Gritty Lasagna Philosophy and the Nexus Model to provide you a way to achieve your personal success...*because grit matters.*

INTRODUCTION

 The purpose for writing this book is to help individuals be the best person they wish to be and to achieve all the success they desire. The problem is when I say the word success, I get responses like, "that's shallow" or "you're missing the point." I'm really not. I mean exactly that, success. Success is only what an individual deems it to be; and while one person may view success as driving around in a luxury car and living in a big, fancy house, others may view it as being a loving spouse and/or parent. The point is not to debate what is and is not success, it is to help people identify their dream and achieve their desired goals- in other words, success.

When I was younger, I considered success as an accumulation of material wealth, an achievement of academic goals and advancement in career status. Fast-forward to present time and I have a very different view of what success is. Success for me now is just about being happy and living my life with a feeling of contentment and gratitude. My point, success looks and feels different to each and every one of us, because our measurement of success is determined by a set of criteria that we each have personally established. As we reach certain goals, our level of success in life will change. As one set of goals is reached, we create new goals for the next level of achievement we desire; this process leads us through life, striving for financial security, academic accreditation, a reciprocal loving relationship, a life full of happiness, and so on.

People have varying beliefs about success, in general. Some think that if a person is successful, that it was just meant to be, while some believe that a person's past dictates their future. Then you have others that believe that success is all about who you know. Maybe there is some truth in some of this, but those who have found the most success in life, are those who understand the concept of GRIT. They understand that the power and ability to succeed comes from within our very being, and that it takes work and dedication to our life goals to achieve. As we continue to talk about success, be clear: success will be different for everyone. How we define success is very specific and very personal, and as we talk about desires, I encourage you to substitute your version of success.

How To Use This Book

This book is written for those interested in personal development and written in a style that is non-conventional. It is intended to offer support by providing tools and techniques with a fun, light approach. We hope that you read it from cover to cover, but this book is written so that when opened to any page, the reader can get something of value. Either way works just fine, and if you are looking for something specific, check out the table of contents.

The depth and breadth of personal development has its downside, too, of course. Exploration of every nook and cranny of who we truly are must be explored and the reader should make a commitment, and invest effort to master his or her personal best. Whether a novice or more experienced in the area of personal development, this book will offer insight. Whenever we can, we sneak in a useful tip or an interesting technique to help you with your needs.

Book Specifics

This book is broken down into chapters that represent specific concepts. Each chapter concept is discussed in general and then broken down into sections and subsections to offer a more detailed account.

Personal Stories:
Each chapter begins with a personal story from one of the two authors. An image is placed next to each story to identify which author is the storyteller. We provide the personal stories to support the chapter point, and to show that we work the techniques discussed in this book every day, too. At times, the reader will find an additional story within the chapter content. We hope that all will enjoy the stories and find value in their meaning.

Scenarios:
The scenarios offer real life situations that support the specific topic discussed. These stories are told through our Gritty Lasagna characters who provide insight in a fun way.

Sketches and Comic Strips:
Visual sketch photos have callouts to specific steps or important concepts discussed throughout the book. They provide a quick visual to reinforce chapter topics.

Quotes:
We love quotes! Several quotes are provided in each chapter to provide a quick perspective of the chapter theme.

Activities:
Each chapter offers activities that support the chapter concepts and provides opportunity for the reader to put the information into action. We encourage the reader to do the activities and hope they find them useful in their personal development quest.

Grit Tips:
Throughout the book, we offer important tips that are included to help us get grittier. Since these tips are helping us build grit, we can consider ourselves under construction. These practical tips will assist in strengthening areas that need some reinforcement.

ICONS, IMAGES AND CHARACTERS IN THE BOOK

While perusing this book, the reader will notice some icons beckoning for attention. Please do not ignore them; embrace them. These icons point out fun, useful, and memorable tidbits about the chapter concepts that are extremely useful.

Grit Tip:

This icon indicates tools, tips and techniques to help build grit in ourselves.

Activities:

This icon indicates activities that put the concepts into action for building.

This icon represents stories presented by Laurie, Co-Author

This icon represents stories presented by Joyce, Co-Author

Throughout this book, we will introduce a group of characters for our scenarios. The reader will see these characters at the time we present a scenario of real life situations to consider.

The next place to go...turn the pages of the book and embrace the topics and concepts presented for the benefit of all.

Gritty Lasagna: The Print in Blueprint

SUCCESS

When I say, "It's like riding a bike", I am referring to the concept that once you learn how to do ride a bike—you never forget; but try sitting on a bike with your feet on the pedals without moving. This is very difficult because it's hard to balance on a bike without movement. Just like in life, it's almost impossible to acquire a feeling of balance without action. Even pedaling a bike at a very slow pace will keep the bike up, balanced, and moving. The pedaling can be slow but it needs to be consistent. While I was learning how to ride a bike as a child, I had many moments of inconsistencies, which always ended up the same way: me on the ground. As with any new venture there are many failures, but if I had given up I would have never experienced all the things I did as a kid. I can remember the first time I rode my bike without training wheels. My father was teaching me. He told me to focus on a point down the road and just keep pedaling, as he proceeded to push me down a mountain. It was actually a very small hill but it felt like a mountain at five years old. I was terrified. I gripped those handle bars until my little knuckles were white, focused on the house straight down the road, and pedaled like I was competing in the Tour de France. I don't remember the number of times I fell before achieving my goal of riding my bike easily without training wheels; I just remember how I felt once I achieved it. I didn't feel scared anymore; I felt free! It was a "good" feeling which I might have described as happy, content, joy, excited, peaceful, and the list goes on. I use that five-year-old feeling as a guide for my life. I continued riding my bike from that day on. It was my primary mode of transportation until I was well into my teenage years. I lived near the beach so there were several drawbridges, which meant I was one of the first ones over the bridge on my bike each day. It was freedom! I used my bike everyday for hours in the summer. My friends and I felt so comfortable on a bicycle that we could ride a lot of the time hands free. We would load up several people on one bike, usually with no shoes and certainly no helmets; it was the 70's & 80's. Throughout the process my initial feeling of fear was replaced with a feeling of freedom and control, and I got to these feelings through practice, and by practice alone. Success in any area in your life is like riding a bike…balance comes through movement and practice. Once you master it, you will not forget it. Now it is time to find a spot on the horizon, focus on it and keep pedaling.

> *Life is like riding a bicycle. In order to keep your balance, you must keep moving."*
> – Albert Einstein

WHAT IS SUCCESS?

What is Success? This question creates a lot of different responses. Success is a word that humans understand, but the concept actually means something different to each and every one of us. Some believe success is a feeling, while others believe success describes a large accomplishment. Some focus their thoughts about success in only specific aspects of life, such as a job, but many people apply the idea of success across all parts of life. This is concerning, because a pattern of accomplishment is regulated by one's definition of success? In simplest terms, success is whatever an individual deems it to be. It is individually defined, and that individual alone determines what success is. So if we only define success in one life area such as a career, what happens to the other segments of our life? Do we not have successes outside of careers? This leads me to ask, "Are we recognizing all the success we are actually achieving?"

Balancing Success

Achieving success in a specific area of our life such as a personal career is wonderful and this type of accomplishment produces feelings of thankfulness and appreciation. These feelings are so rewarding that once a success, such as a promotion is achieved, immediately feelings such as satisfaction and contentment are experienced. We realize that we like feeling this way so we create a new career goal to accomplish, because we want experience this feeling again. We liked feeling this way. So if these feelings of accomplishment are so wonderful, why do many people narrowly focus the concept of success in only this one area of life instead of contemplating success into broader terms? Are we missing the big picture?

Our life can be the reward of striving for overall balance, and that balance can reflect our focus of wide-ranging success in our entire life. Success is not just achieved by the things that we can see. Inner achievements are those things that are invisible to the outside world, and many times are the areas where  individuals have the greatest successes. Remember, we create our own definition of success, so do not be afraid to fall short of this triumph. By falling short, we are at least reaching high. When I teach my college success course, I always tell my students, "Reach for the moon. Even if you fall short and land amongst the stars, is that not higher than you are right now?" Why not dream big? Dreaming big and setting higher goals for oneself allow an individual to achieve beyond their current state. It may seem as if we are identifying a success that is so grand that it may seem unattainable. Maybe it is, but only one person truly knows that answer. The purpose of dreaming big is not to have us create lofty goals, but to create a mindset that believes that it is possible. We alone are the only one who knows how much effort we are willing to exert to get to that pot of gold at the end of the rainbow. Some may be skeptical, but what if we do attain this goal, and get to the pot of gold? How would that feel? Is it not worth trying or does the fear of failure stop us in our tracks? The concept of failure alone should not determine if we pursue our dreams. Why? Because falling short of these grand goals will still bring us many successes in life and moves us further than we can ever expected. If we expect great success across the board, in all that we do today and throughout life, we will achieve great success. No one on this earth deserves anything more than any other person.

Success is connected with action. Successful people keep moving. They make mistakes, but they never quit. –Conrad Hilton

ILLUSION OF SUCCESS

If we personally define success, then why do so many people consider themselves failures? Low self-esteem, unrealistic expectations, negative self talk are all contributing factors, but the main reason is because most people think success looks like this…

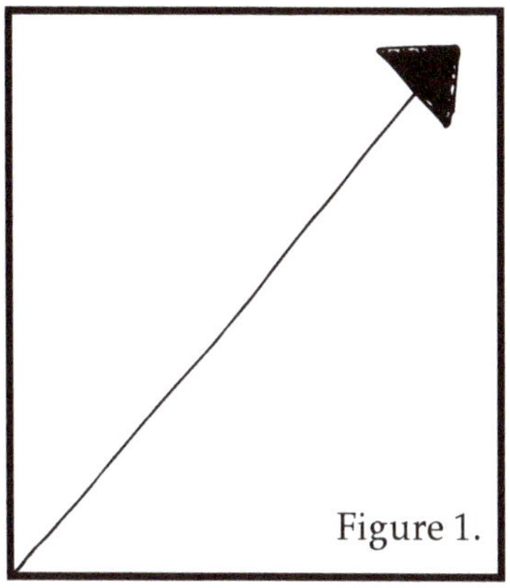

BUT

But success really looks like this…

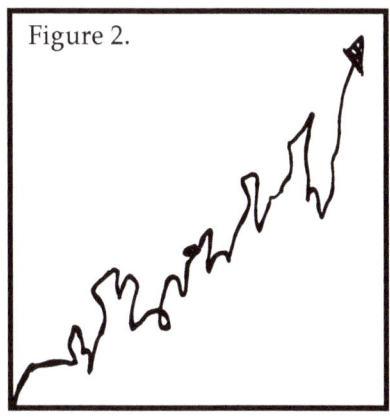

Figure 1.

Figure 2.

The path to success belief that most individuals have is an illusion.

FAILURE IS KEY

The work of Paul Tough, whose books *How Children Succeed* and *Whatever it Takes* challenge the hypothesis that success depends primarily on cognitive skills by presenting the thought that IQ is key to success. His books discuss the notion that non-cognitive skills, like persistence, self-control, curiosity, resilience, and grit are more crucial than sheer brainpower to achieving success.

"Character is created by encountering and overcoming failure," he states, and he even suggests the question, "What if the secret of success is failure?" Maybe this should be repeated. What if the Secret of Success is Failure? To cultivate the quality of GRIT, we should learn and understand how to cope with disappointment and defeat. We must recognize that it is a point in time and does not define who we are. It is merely a learning opportunity. The timeless and uncomfortable truth is that encountering and overcoming failure almost always forge true strength of character. No one is exempt from the school of hard knocks. The key is how we respond to such setbacks. Do we lose heart, or do we learn things about ourselves? Do we blame others or do we change our approach? Do we become more skittish or find a way to bounce back?

Steve Jobs noted in his famous commencement speech at Stanford in 2005, "Sometimes life hits you in the head with a brick." Jobs had revolutionized the world of personal computers in 1984 with the Macintosh, but then the project faltered, and he was fired from the very company he had founded. "It was awful-tasting medicine," he said, "but I guess the patient needed it." Jobs concluded that getting fired was actually the best thing that could have happened to him. Why? Jobs said it was because it drove him to reassess everything, to rekindle his creative fire, and to double his effort and commitment to his goals. It made him resilient. It made him gritty.

Failure provides great knowledge and is just part of one's journey to success. It is part of life. When Thomas Edison was inventing the light bulb he tried over 100 different ways before he found success. He stated that he didn't make 100 mistakes. He learned 100 ways not to make a light bulb. He understood the value in failure. Mr. Edison was able to learn what worked and what did not, and used this information to his advantage to invent a device that revolutionized the world. No one will live life without experiencing failure, but those of us who can see failure as an opportunity will achieve greater rewards. Each of us have the power to achieve all of our life's dreams...the power to create the exact life we want, but this should be understood that without failure, success will not exist.

Got Grit?

The definition of insanity is doing the same thing over and over and expecting a different result."
- Albert Einstein

100% of failures started with an action of doing. Trying something new can be a scary thought, but the fear of failure should not keep one from trying. If we are not doing, then nothing will ever get accomplished. One thing to consider: the laws that govern failure do not discriminate regardless of age, sex, weight, skin color or personal appearance. None of this makes a difference, because at one time or another every single one of us will fail at something.

If we are going to survive unexpected circumstances and disappointments, we have to be willing to change, adjust, work with our strengths and commit to some things we normally would not choose to do. Despite our best efforts and intentions, we may fall short because we do not know the direction we are going. If we begin the journey with a clear dream for our future and put in place effective short-term and long-term goals to get there, we have a better chance of obtaining everything we want in life.

"Hope deferred makes the heart sick" simply means when things do not go the way we hoped, we may want to quit and walk away with disappointment and a broken heart. This is a huge mistake. Wrenched with displeasure, we feel bad and if we keep choosing to walk away, it will not be long before we are hurt, distressed and ultimately filled with regret. We all hate to lose. No one ever says, " I am so excited about failing!" But maybe we should. The problem is that we cannot comprehend why it would be a good thing to fail, because we do not look at failure as the opportunity it is. When we begin to redirect our opinions about failure, we can start to understand the value and the learning opportunity that lies within each disappointment.

By accepting a different view, we start to learn from our mistakes, and our eyes are open to other avenues once closed off. If we pull the best ideas from each failed opportunity, we will have a better chance of achieving success. Achieving success opens us to new hills to climb, seas to cross, and experiences to conquer. With each failure that ultimately results in success, we are building grit. But how do we keep fighting when we feel disappointed, offended and inept? We do it by engaging in conscious, deliberate actions fueled by thoughts of achievement and reward. We are no longer driven by insecurity, defeat, and those pesky thoughts that shine a spotlight on our past mistakes. No one is perfect and without flaws. When we make mistakes or fail, the tendency can be to beat ourselves up long after the moment has passed. When we stop condemning ourselves for past failures, and understand the connection that our thoughts and emotions have on our actions and behaviors, when we experiences failure, we can recognize that it is only a moment in time. Failure is inevitable; doesn't the idea that we are not perfect and that we cannot expect to be, give us some relief? If so, then why is this fear of failure still holding so many back.

Most of us would like to think that we are gritty, but how gritty are we, really? Are we willing to get into the thick of it, get down and dirty and do whatever is needed to reach our goals? If we are honest, we can all remember moments in our lives when we gave up, stopped short of achieving success. Why?

A. Did we not understand what steps were required?
B. Did we not want to fail?
C. Did we not want to do the work?
D. Did we not demonstration the behaviors needed?
E. All of the above.

Grit = Success

When the decision was made to write this book, we considered many factors that represented our philosophy on how to develop one's self into the best Self a person can be. Helping others achieve personal growth clearly resonated as our overall goal. And as we examined the many important concepts of realizing that growth, it became clear that no matter what factor we used, any individual development is ultimately a success and to obtain this personal growth, an individual would need to embrace the idea that change would be needed and the desire to persevere would have to be present. Without the willingness to embrace change and the inability to sustain stamina, successful growth is unattainable. Ultimately, we need grit and change to achieve any goal. Think about it. If grit and change are not needed, then of course, it is because in this particular capacity of our life, we already consider it to be an area of achieved success. If we are not totally satisfied with ourselves, but we are not willing to be gritty and make changes, then thinking success will magically appear is insane.

If some type of change were not needed, then we would have already achieved the results we want, correct? This is why success really looks like the squiggly line in figure 2. Success is a long path where we make great strides, as well as experience those moments of sliding backwards down steep hills. When we make great strides, we keep doing things the same way. Why, because it is working! It is at that moment when we slide backwards that we must re-examine what changes need to be made. What we were doing was not allowing us to move forward on our quest. To keep from falling any further behind, we should consider an alternate plan to minimize obstacles that keep us from making forward progress. By embracing the understanding that achieving personal growth is not a final destination, but actually an ongoing journey, we recognize that it is the lessons that we learn along way that really determine our personal success.

WHAT COMES FIRST...THE CHICKEN OR THE EGG?

So what comes first… success or happiness? Same idea as what comes first, the chicken or the egg? Only we will be able to answer that question for our self, but by developing our life's plan around the whole person, we can devise a plan that consists of our hopes and dreams. The Nexus Model, explained in the next chapter, will act as a blueprint to achieve our goals that will bring us happiness and success.

Does success lead to happiness or does happiness cause success? When we see the demise of a wealthy famous person we raise our eyebrows and nod at the TV and mumble "yup, money doesn't make you happy." We know that cognitively, but many times the very next thing that comes out of our mouth is "I would love to have their "problems" if I had their money." Someone's financial success obviously doesn't lead him or her to be happy (we know at least one well off person that is miserable). If we understand that an achievement itself doesn't necessarily have long term lingering effects on our happiness then why do we put our happiness on hold for when we get _____ or achieve_____ (fill in the blanks).

There is a retirement community in California where many of the residents live into their late 90's and beyond. Researchers wanted to know why and started gathering information to determine the factors that aided in their long lives. One of the main prevailing characteristics of these individuals that lived the longest was happiness. These individuals are happy and choose to be happy every day. They enjoy their lives, they moderately exercise up to 45 minutes a day, they drink up to 2 glasses of wine a day, and they keep moving their mind and body being guided by happiness. They value their lives and are in it for the long haul and not just grunting it out in short spurs of misery in hopes of an earth shattering payoff. They are not in a hurry to get their lives over with. They relish life, and decide to live the time they have on this earth in a positive, happy place. They cannot understand why anyone would want to live life any other way. Isn't the universal goal to have the highest quality of life for the longest period of time?

There is nothing wrong with achieving things and being successful, but what good is it if we are not happy, satisfied, content, joyful, peaceful, etc. We want to be guided by those types of feelings. We remember emotionally charged situations whether they create positive or negative feelings because humans are emotional beings. Some of the most vivid memories we have bring back a surge of emotion when these memories pop into our mind. Feelings are powerful. The things we choose to pursue in our lives can be determined by how we feel, so we want our desired life feeling to assist us in building the life we want. We will know best if we are on our path by the way we feel.

Happiness is ultimately the overall feeling, whether riding our bike gives us a feeling of freedom or inventing the light bulb provides us the feeling of accomplishment, we feel happy. The feeling could be joy, appreciation, contentment, peace, etc. Whatever we chose as our descriptive word as our overall life's feeling, or *Cinque (chin-kway)* is personal, and we choose it because it makes us happy. Happiness is a major factor in the quality of our life. Put focus on the idea of creating happiness, creating that personal *Cinque*, and letting that life feeling guide us. To create the life we want we will create actions that will get us there, and it is easier when we are guided by our *Cinque*. Surround ourselves with people who love and support us and who emulate our *Cinque*. By understanding who we are right now and where we plan to go, others can help us stay on track. We need these people on our journey to achieve our stated goals; however, it's up to us to request their support and be specific about how they can play a role in our success. Surround yourself with happy people, because happiness is contagious.

> "People will forget what you said. People will forget what you did. But people will never forget how you made them feel." – Bob Kelly

CINQUE

Most of us have, at one time or another, fanaticized about what we would like to have in life. As a child, dreams flourish in our minds consistently, and we designate a vision of what will make us happy when 'we grow up'. As an adult, we reflect back on those early visions and modify them along the way, but have we ever thought about what success would feel like? What sensation would consume us upon achieving our goals and dreams? What daily emotion compels gratification in our lives? Until I was having a conversation years ago with my co-author, I never gave much attention to the emotions that were aroused when I envisioned or attained a goal; I only considered the visual as significant. Let me tell you, if I had recognized the feeling and emotion identified with success, I believe that I would have acknowledged long ago that I have been consistently achieving success throughout my entire

life. I was experiencing success after success, but because it was not a large goal or my big life dream, I discounted those moments and did not see them as accomplishments. I failed to see that those smaller achievements were stepping-stones and vital to the success I experience today. Individuals have a tendency to overlook the small triumphs in life and only acknowledge the grand victories. In addition, we seem to have difficulty letting go of the small hiccups, slumps and failures experienced. We need to exchange the focus that we place on our failures and shine that attention on our many daily successes. We all experience some type of success every day, but many of us miss these moments, because we have not identified success with a feeling. Without our *Cinque*, we tend to miss these opportunities to pat ourselves on the back.

We must challenge ourselves to find the emotions, our *Cinque*, that gives us comfort and joy, and bring those emotions into our daily lives. Stay aware and keep our *Cinque* in the forefront of our mind and allow it to point us in the direction of our goals, while we enjoy each moment of our lives in positive state of minds. *Cinque* is that feeling that we want to experience every day, and by which we gauge our current emotional state. If joy is one of our designated *Cinque*, then joy is the emotion we strive each day to feel. As we participate in our daily activities and have interactions with others, we need to strive for finding the joy in those experiences. When we strive to find the joy in all we do, and make our decisions that are in alignment with our goals, success is found.

ACTIVITY

A Life Worth Living

Identify your Life Feeling, or better known as in our book, as your Cinque. Identify the 5 feelings that you want to define and guide your life. Ask yourself, "When I am at the end the days on this earth and I reflect back on my life, what 5 core feelings do I want to be consistently present in my life throughout my time here on earth?" Think of significant events in your life and the positive feelings that your experienced in those moments that you would like to carry with you. Think of the feelings that you want to represent your journey, describe your life story, fill your Nexus home.

1. _____
2. _____
3. _____
4. _____
5. _____

It's Not Just Rainbows and Unicorns

Happiness and success are something individuals pursue. The best moments and achievements in a person's life do not transpire because we were doing nothing more than waiting for their arrival, so we can ride on our unicorn to find the pot of gold at the end of the rainbow. Someone who experiences happiness and success does not do so because opportunities just fell from the sky, and were the lucky one that received this rain shower of good fortune. We cannot expect to lie in bed all day staring at the ceiling and have happiness or success come knocking on our door. If it could happen that easily, people would walk around without umbrellas every time the weather report said there was a chance of rain.

Some people may disagree, and think that fate is at play. Fate states that certain events are predetermined and that individuals have no power or control when these events occur. Fate is different from having faith. Faith is a strong trust, conviction, or belief in something that is not tangible. "It happens for a reason", comes out of my mouth quite often. When events occur that are out of my control, I chose to believe in faith, not fate. I chose to believe that there is a purpose, a lesson, a meaning for these bumps in the road that have appeared. I choose to believe that although I cannot control any event, I can control how I react to the event. I can control what I do with these feelings, and I control how long I allow these feelings to reside in my body.

Faith is a concept that can be difficult for some to grasp. The inability to trust in something intangible can be hard. To move forward and open ourselves to new experiences and new people we must let go of anything that isn't working in our life. It takes conviction and self-belief to move forward with faith guiding the way. Faith is a coping mechanism that gives an individual control over an event where there is no real control, while being fateful puts us in the position of being a victim. Faith makes us more aware of what is available to lead and guide us in a positive direction. If we practice consistently and let go of the things that are not adding value to our lives, we generate the self-worth and self-reliance required to make that leap of faith.

Let's just say for a moment that success and happiness do rain down upon certain people because they are the lucky, chosen ones. Ok, so when we do not find ourselves in the fateful rainstorm, we still have the power to control our destiny. In simple terms, if we want happiness we can pursue it. If we want success, we can pursue it. We are not locked out of these types of achievement just because fate has not chosen us.

Family, work, school, relationships move along steadily and at times it feels like when one area falls out of sync, the others soon follow. Life is rolling by and then within a ten-day period, this happy, peaceful life that we have come to enjoy, becomes a part of turmoil and strife. It starts by the oldest child moving out of their college apartment, and will be home from school for the summer while taking online courses. Another child is in a fender bender with one of the family cars. Our spouse is working day and night dealing with a significant issue that has arisen at their workplace, and an opportunity comes out of nowhere for us to make some extra money taking on a second job that can be done at home.

As we travel through this time period, the oldest child being home for the summer changes the family dynamics, and the 3 youngest children, usually very obedient, start to mimac the oldest child's behavior, which is ok for a twenty year old, but not for an eleven, twelve, and sixteen year old to exhibit. Due to the recent fender bender, the parent taxi has been re-commissioned and due to our spouse's work crisis, they are working late every day and are not able to share the load of taxi driver. Even the oldest child is not able to help with the chauffeuring the other children around due to the online schoolwork they are now doing. Quickly, it becomes apparent that our time to work on this new money making opportunity is significantly reduced, and the impact of the limited time available is effecting our ability to meet previous work deadlines that were in place prior to taking on this new work at home venture The stress level of all the individuals in the home is rising, although everyone is doing their best to not flip out. The lack of communication occurring because everyone is trying to stay to themselves to limit the negative interactions with one another is causing more problems than it is solving. Within a few short days, life is turned upside down. The problem is that over a short period of time we continue feeling stressed and bothered, even though the kids are getting where they need to go, our spouse has time to deal with their work crisis, and we are working hard at our two money making jobs. Upon reflection, we ponder why the looming negativity exists. Should we not be feeling better that the goals are being met, and that we have handled the stones that life has recently thrown at us? Then the proverbial light bulb goes off. Although we were going through the motions, we were looking at these stones as a fateful event. They are happening and there is nothing we can do. At some level that is correct. We cannot go back in time and change the events that have brought us to this place, but we can be aware of ourselves. Focus on the steps we are taking to leads us to a more positive outcome. When we have faith in ourselves, we can see the positive and our actions become more enlightened and more in line with our thinking. Looking at the positives of each situation and creating a positive pattern of thinking our reality for changed for the better.

- Our child is home from college and we get to spend more time with them
- At least our spouse still has a job even though it requires him to work long hours for the next few weeks
- A car is available to transport the children everywhere they need to go, and get me to and from work
- The insurance company is going to pay for the damage caused during the fender bender.
- We have a second job that is bringing extra money into the home.

We should create a proactive plan that assissts in achieving all our goals. We have our eyes on the prize, and feel good about the plan that will keep us on track during this crazy period in life. Once we start reflecting on the positives of the situation we can be happier. We no longer feel like a victim of fate, we have become the architect of what is to come, and we have changed our thinking to focus on the positives of the situations and not dwell on the negatives. This shift in thinking immediatley lightens our spirits, and the feeling of gratitude reveals the joys and happiness in the situation. Our *Cinque* is now the driving force, and when kept in the forefront of our minds, these feelings can easily bring us back to a path that not only helps us reach our goals, but allows us to enjoy the journey, as well.

Success is here for us all. No matter how big or small the accomplishment, it is still success. Appreciate every moment of every day, and choose to live guided by our *Cinque*. Stay tuned in to our emotions and limit the negative feelings from encompassing our body. By knowing where we are going, losing the fear of failure, adding the gritty mindset, and allowing our *Cinque* to guide us, we will achieve success in life. It is as easy as riding a bike. In the next few chapters, the Nexus Model is presented to provide guidance for building a blueprint to achieve our life goals. Grit is a byproduct of our success.

THE NEXUS CONNECTION

When I'm teaching my students about how their brain works I use the analogy of Facebook. I joined Facebook not knowing what Facebook was…I know I was living under a rock. I received an email from Facebook inviting me to see my friend's pictures. When I clicked on the link I was bombarded with people's names I haven't seen in years. Do you know? Jen, Steve, Debbie, and the list went on. I clicked yes, yes, and yes…not knowing I was then reconnected to all these people I haven't seen since high school or college. I quickly understood the inter-workings of Facebook, and as an observer, I noticed those who had the most Facebook friends, those who enjoyed commenting on "friends" posts, and those who were "LIKING" everything from a cute kid photo to a serious international social problem. Through repeated usage these expert Facebookers were now in the daily lives of one another and in many respects making life easier for one another. Expert learners know that it is important to repeatedly cause similar firings of neurons to result in long-term memory. The more we talk to a friend on Facebook or solve similar math problems the stronger the connection; if you make no contact after making that first click with that high school acquaintance or don't touch a math book after class then this connection is weak. Little or no progress is made with weak or even broken connections. We can take a plethora of actions like staring at a math book for hours and copying notes, but without any correlation to the task at hand there is minimal growth and understanding. Everything in life is about making connections. Strong connections whether neural or relational make learning easier and provide needed social support. Making connections matter to human beings- physiologically and socially. Connections can change the quality of our learning and relationships.

The mind is like a parachute. It only works when open. –Albert Einstein

THE SECRET INGREDIENT

Looking around, we see a number of successful people and wonder, "How did they achieve it?" We come up with statements like, they must be lucky or it must be fate. I promise you, it was not fate or luck that provided these individuals with the success they achieved. It is GRIT. Many have the wrong impression of how success is achieved. Success is considered to look like a straight arrow heading up in figure 1. in the last chapter, but in reality, success looks very different. On a path to success there are many stumbles and falls that occur alongside small and large gains.

Think about some of the more renowned people in the history, for example, Steve Jobs and Mohammad Gandhi. These individuals are consistently successful, but some may have a belief that they rose to the top without faults, mistakes, hardships or disappointments. This is because the result we see is these two men at the top of Success Mountain. Unless we are close to these individuals, we are not privy to the long, difficult road they have traveled. We missed the part where obstacles stood in their way more than a few times, including moments when they were knocked down so hard, that many of us would not want to get back up; but these men did. Why? Because they possessed that special ingredient called grit. Grit is the growth, resilience, integrity, and tenacity to pursue goals and dreams, in spite of obstacles and failures. They understood the power needed to acquire the bigger life dream. They recognized the need to stay on the path of that dream, and were intimately aware of themselves. By being real and honest, they were the creators of their own destinies.

Our Journey Begins

To live the life we desire, we need to visualize that which we want to obtain. This requires us to set goals and targets that are in true alignment with our mind, body and spirit. We must consciously think of the life we want allowing our brain to embrace these thoughts and bring our attention to the connection between what we want, what we think and what we do. We must be mindful. Mindful of the emotions evoked when we have achieved success in the past and mindful of the emotions we evoke when we envision our future life's goals and dreams. If we keep our thoughts, emotions, and actions in alignment, we will accomplish our goals and achieve success repeatedly, ultimately obtaining the life we desire.

It is very common to feel as if our life is passing us by. We wake up and begin our daily routine. We go to work, take care of the family, maintain the house, and before you know it, it is time to go to bed, just to start the whole cycle over again. This pattern is a bit daunting and would make anyone wonder how to live a life chosen, but life is life. There will be moments along the way that are sad, happy, fun, painful and difficult. Life can be full of dark periods, regardless of whether we want them to occur or not. Thank goodness nothing is permanent and being connected to our Cinque keeps us loving along our path, even when those dark periods and other obstacles try to stand in our way. Our blueprint helps provide direction to keep us moving forward, and shape our vision. Guided by our Cinque, the mindfulness to persevere is conscious and we can commit to living life desired.

Many times we are not mindful. We are not engaged in the present moment. When this happens, our muscle memory, brain recollections, and behavioral habits carry us through the day haphazardly. To begin our quest we must draw our attention back to the present and create purpose for our behavior. As we become an active participant in our daily lives, we stay conscious of the commitment to our life's desire, and we exhibit behaviors that are purposeful and perform action toward our goals.

People with grit don't believe failure is a permanent condition."

-Angele Lee Duckworth

ACTIVITY

Pondering Questions

1. What does success look like to you?
2. Have you every really thought about what you want in life? If not, take a moment to develop what this vision looks like.
3. What does your dream include?
4. As you envision your life dream, see this dream in present time; see yourself in the dream, already living your dream. See yourself already achieving the life you desire.
5. Focus attention on how you feel in your dream and identify that emotion, by name and meaning. Was this emotion identified as one of your five emotions representing your Cinque?
6. With this emotion in mind, reflect on other successes you have had, but may not have given full acknowledgement to when they occurred. This emotion is part of your Cinque. These emotions define your life in a positive way, and if used as your driving force, can keep you on your path.

THE SECRET TO GETTING GRITTY

Time to get gritty on the count of three, 1, 2 and 3. Are we now gritty? It is not enough for someone to tell us to get gritty. If it were that easy, the world would look like a very different place. Getting gritty requires a personal, honest awareness, and a willingness to change those things that we allow to stand in our way. We have to commit to make positive change occur because we recognize the connection between our thoughts, feelings and actions. We must embrace the power we possess to create the future we want, and be willing to walk that path for as long as it takes, in spite of temporary failures.

The Nexus model is the special ingredient to building grit. Nexus offers a layered mind map for success, and is comprised of 7 key components. This model is about making connections; how each component connects to our self, to our world and our vision, which ultimately impacts our ability to obtain our goals and achieve success. The Nexus Model helps us look at our personality, habits, behaviors, perception, that impact our life outcomes. By taking a mindful glance at the driving forces of our choices, we can alter our current paths to find success.

The Nexus Model shows us how to launch and sustain a holistic approach to personal change by supporting and empowering individuals to pursue their life's desires and overcome obstacles that can stand in the way. This approach is something that can simply and easily be incorporated in our life as much or as little as one is prepared to embrace. There are many options available in this book to assist us on our journey to acquire the success we desire and make the personal changes required. By identifying little steps we can do each day, by focusing our effort in small ways, we can begin to see how achievable positive change can be.

Acquiring and maintaining a positive feeling towards behavior change takes some work, but by taking little steps based on the 7 components of the model, progress can be made. The Nexus model is an ongoing process. The connection that each component has to each other and to our individual self strengthen as we build these connections in our daily lives. Change can be a very scary thought for some and it can be extremely uncomfortable to get real with ourselves when we examine inward. What better place to step out on the proverbial ledge than in the comfort of our own home? Home is a safe place. Home can be a place where we can fail and not be embarrassed or ashamed. At home we can be open, honest and real; we can be our true selves. This is extremely important, because until we are willing to look at ourselves intimately and acknowledge "our stuff", we cannot make the needed changes. Applaud the inner strengths that will lead us toward obtaining our short-term, long-term and life goals.

Home Sweet Home

Building a house will serve as our safe place, our man cave (women cave), our little oasis, or whatever we want to call it, as this will play an important role in releasing any fears or inhibitions that we may be experiencing about this process. By understanding the importance of each component of the Nexus Model, we can recognize the areas in our lives that may need some alterations. Each area discussed plays an important role in our total and complete self and without a strong grasp on the components in the model, the struggle to reach our goals is intensified. Just like building a house, if one of the sections of our house is weak, the structure as a whole is faltered.

UNDERSTANDING THE NEXUS MODEL COMPONENTS

The components of the model are simple. It is the simplicity that allows individuals to build grit along the way and achieve success. The following definition analogies will help you easily identify the importance of each component.

Self-Awareness is the foundation of our house. This is what supports all the other building materials. A strong foundation is needed and without its strength the house will fall down.

Social Awareness is the walls of a house. The walls combined with the foundation create support for the roof. It plays a fundamental part of a house's structure and repairs must be made when cracks are visible to keep the walls from crumbling.

Emotional Intelligence is the roof of a house. The roof protects the house from the elements. If the roof is damaged, this damage allows the appliances and furnishings in our house to be damaged by exposing them to the elements.

Stress Management is the windows of a house. Stress makes our vision cloudy when not dealt with in a functional way. The windows of our house show our vision to the outside world clear or blurred, and if we allow stress to overcome us, we can blow our windows out causing damage to ourselves, as well as those around us by the broken glass fragments.

Communication Strategies are the doors of a houses. Communication is the access between the inside and outside world. Like the door to our house, it is the gateway to others.

Choice is the appliances, furnishings, etc. This concept represents the tools we need to make our house comfortable. The furnishings, appliances, etc., that are needed to help us get through life more easily. When our appliances are not functioning properly or if the leg of our couch is broken, some type of change must take place to bring things back to our Cinque. Without the ability to use our tools, we soon are living in a chaotic state.

Life Plan is the sidewalk to and from our house. The path that will lead us to places we want to go; the stepping-stones that will lead us to reaching our goals, obtaining our dreams, and achieving success.

Try to stay positive about your past and present. Dwelling on things that cannot be changed does nothing to keep you moving forward. What was, was. What is, is. What can be is up to you, embrace change for the future.

Is That a Backhoe I Hear?

Are we ready to build our house of grit? The following chapters break down the Nexus Model and go through each concept area with clear explanations and enlightening activities to build on our individual strengths. Our goal is to present the information in a fun, encouraging manner offering positive inspiration to take what we already have and make repairs to our house that we want, instead of living with cracks in the house's structure, over time, will end up with a condemned sign posted on the door, if repairs are not made. Each individual will determine their own starting point, and modify a life blueprint to obtain designated personal goals. As we walk our path, tools will be offered to assist us when we hit those bumps in the road that can knock us off our planned course. Nexus identifies basic areas to reach our full potential by building personal grit along the way. Each approach to this process will differ from one person to the next, so embrace the opportunity to create a personalized and customized blueprint.

This view of "our" house represents the way we would like to view ourselves and how we want the world to see us. Our curb appeal creates a perception of what is going on inside the house whether it is true or not.

What we see depends mainly on what we look for. – John Lubbock

This view of "our" house represents the actual, present state of ourselves which may or may not be visible to the outer world. If we never take a good look at ourselves and develop the skills presented in the Nexus Model, we may not realize the damaging long-term effects the outside world can have.

If you are ready to proceed, then hit the "Like" button and turn the page.

Self-Awareness

Self-Awareness is the foundation to our house. This is what supports all the other building materials. A strong foundation is needed and without its strength the house can fall down.

SELF-AWARENESS

A long time ago in a college course, I was asked to describe myself in three words. I said, "I...Don't... Know!" The whole class erupted into laughter, and my instructor looked un-amused at my comment, and told me she would come back to me for an answer. To be honest, I was trying to be funny, because the question caught me off guard. I was astonished at the realization that I did not have an answer. How could I not have three words to describe myself? Because the question had taken aback, I stumbled over what to say. This was one of those moments when I was quick and witty, making the people around me laugh at my 'funny', but the only problem, I was not just being funny. I was being honest and truthful. I really did not know. I had never taken the time to think about it. I could easily find words that were based on my physical appearances to described myself such as, brunette, brown eyes, tall, but those words could be applied to millions of people around the world. The question asked was to identify three words that described my uniqueness, three words that described myself at my core. As I reflected to identify my descriptive words, when a word popped into my mind that had a negative connotation, I ignored it, and would search for one that I considered more positive. When the instructor came back to me for an answer, I gave her the first three positive words that came to my mind presenting myself in a positive light to my classmates. As the instructor continued the lesson, I quickly realized that this question was asked to see how well I knew myself, but even more important, this question was asked to see how honest I could be about the person I really am. Those first words that popped into my head that I considered negative, came flooding back into the forefront of my mind. It hit me. I knew who I was, but certain aspects of who I was, did not thrill me. I wanted to ignore these parts of my personality that I did not like, and hoped that if I didn't acknowledge them, they would go away. I quickly understood there was only one thing I could do; embrace these characteristics and work on making positive change to those areas that I was trying to ignore. Now years later, I can easily identify my three words, and am open with who I am, but only because I was asked that one particular question all those years ago.

> *What is necessary to change a person is to change his awareness of himself.* –Abraham Maslo

THREE WORDS

The dictionary is full of words. Many descriptive words could be used to describe individuals, their personalities, their behaviors, and their characteristics. These simple words say so much in just a few letters. Unfortunately, many of those words are never used or even known outside of the pages where they are written, but those are the words we should strive to find. Those are the words that are the most descriptive and telling about who we really are. We must give some attention to this question posed. What words create a clear, objective vision of whom we are when given to others? What words truly describe us individually? It is time to find out.

ACTIVITY

My Model

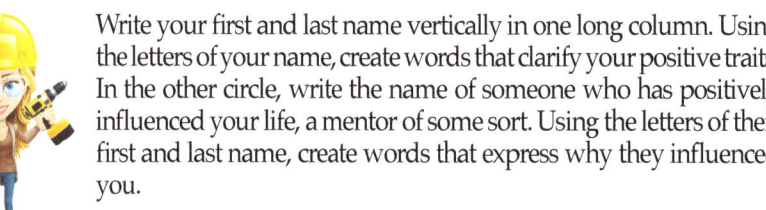

Write your first and last name vertically in one long column. Using the letters of your name, create words that clarify your positive traits. In the other circle, write the name of someone who has positively influenced your life, a mentor of some sort. Using the letters of their first and last name, create words that express why they influenced you.

When doing this exercise, use the first word that pops into your mind when you see the letter, but make sure it is truly a descriptor word of you and your mentor.

YOU	MENTOR

If you lack Self-Awareness you can't change. Why should you? As far as you're concerned, you are doing EVERYTHING right." – Jim Whitt

What words did you use? Were the words you chose positive or negative? Did you find that your descriptor words chosen for your mentor were similar or different than the words you chose for yourself? Were you surprised by any of the words you chose? Do you think the words you wrote down are a true representation of the real you? Now that you are starting to think about this, what are your three words that describe you and all or your uniqueness?

WHAT IS SELF-AWARENESS?

We are who we are. We are wonderful beings that volunteer at our child's schools, build homes for the homeless, cheer on our favorite football team whether they win or lose, and always take life with a grain of salt…maybe with a slice of lemon, a ring of salt and a shot of tequila, too, every once in a while. Many are just not inclined to spend much time on self-reflection. It is easier to take the tequila shot and move on. Even when feedback is presented to us, we are not always open to it. Honest feedback is not always flattering. Consequently, many people have low self-awareness, which is the reason why the self-help book genre is booming. Now, before we start getting frustrated or feeling badly about ourselves, remember everyone has things about themselves that they don't particularly like, even the most successful individuals. We all have something that we would like to change, but we cannot fix what we don't know or admit. Successful people acknowledge the good, the bad, and the ugly (I think I hear Clint Eastwood's spurs clinking). This is the reason these people are so successful. They build on their strengths and have learned what is necessary to prevail over those areas that could pull them in another direction. They are self-aware. Recognition is key and just like the first step in the AA Twelve Step Program, we are admitting that we have a problem. Well, maybe not actually a problem, but you get the point. Personal growth is needed to achieve success, but success is not as simple as the definition in the Webster Dictionary: a favorable or desired outcome: the attainment of wealth, favor, or eminence. Success is ultimately living our life in our own way. But what does that really mean?

It means identifying our hopes, dreams, and goals for a life we desire and taking the steps to start walking down the path towards obtaining what we actually want. So what are the life goals, dreams, hopes we have? We do not have to identify them now…that comes later, but start thinking about it. What is it that we really want today, tomorrow, next month, for life? Maybe someone out there would like to lose 20 pounds, but someone else might like to create a closer relationship with their teenage child; maybe another person wants to do a better job of controlling their anger at work. Without excuse, it is time to identify who we are. Whether we make a choice to change something about ourselves or not, the importance is that we position ourselves in alignment with our hopes, dreams, and goals, and start walking that path. Now that we have started to reflect, would you say that you really know yourself?

Self Awareness is having a clear perception of our personality, including strengths, weaknesses, thoughts, beliefs, motivation, and emotions. Understanding one's self can help during arguments, in choosing friends, finding success in school or career, maintaining nourishing relationships, and in finding general peace and joy in life. It sounds straightforward, but it takes some adults years before we understand what this concept means, and how to really apply it to our lives. Being mentally and emotionally present in situations, understanding how our actions affect people, and being clued into what we really enjoy and dislike all equate to have a heightened level of self awareness.

Keep it Real. Be honest with yourself, and don't shy away from the real you. Place focus on your strengths, and find the lesson in all opportunities that present themselves.

SELF-AWARENESS IS LIKE...

Should we build an elevated house out of sticks and thatch if we live in an area that experiences severe thunderstorms, hurricanes or tornados." Why worry about the paint colors, furnishings, pictures, and knick-knacks that make our home enjoyable when, more than likely, the house will all come crashing down during an impending weather event? The best-case scenario is the storms stay small as they come through, but this is wishful thinking if the home is located in tornado alley. A house made of sticks and thatch will be no match for powerful storms that develop in this area, and after the storms hit, we are left with total destruction. It is only a matter of time before a large, extremely powerful storm arrives and levels the house to the ground, leaving us with no choice but to start from scratch to rebuild. Oh goodie, where do I sign?

Even if we make some personal changes, our efforts can slip away as quickly as they appear, if we just do a quick repair job, rather than fortify the structure and its foundation. Avoid building weak walls for our house so that the slightest wind can easily knock them down. If we choose to build in an area that has severe storms and choose to use sticks because they are quick and easier to find, we will be building those walls over and over again, never making any progress on the rest of the house. I don't know about most people, but I would definitely like to know that if I am putting so much effort into building a home, not just a house, that it is going to be around for many years to come. This is no different when it comes to creating a good foundation for our personal growth. If we make a choice to build a strong foundation on solid ground and we use the correct tools and the best materials, we will strengthen the areas that are weak; creating a structure that can withstand anything that comes our way. Personal growth is like a house needing a solid foundation, no different than a rocket needing a stable launching pad. Careful construction is required to ensure that our structure can be supported and self-awareness is the material that creates that strong base.

Take note that even the most well built structures need repair from time to time, but if we keep up with the tiny repairs as they occur, there will be no need to take out a second mortgage on the home due to a huge expense that appears from years of neglect. Self-awareness is not a final goal, but a continual progression needed to further our development process. Even after 20 years of studying human behavior and fully understanding the concept of self-awareness, heightening personal awareness is done each and every day. This concept of awareness is simple, and using it consistently comes easier with practice. Many things in life can change us, cloud our thinking and wreak havoc on our journey for the good or the bad. Once we are more aware, we can take action to create a positive life outlook, and begin taking action to reinforce this stronger foundation.

Self Awareness is the groundwork for changing the emotional quality of our life. It is extremely important and should be considered vital in an individual's ability to achieve any victory, as we need to understand that we can only control ourselves and no one else. We may impact and have influence on others in our life, but we cannot control them at all. Everyone has free will, and each one of us needs a firm grasp of who we are before we can confidently move forward to achieve success, experience our cinque, and find peace of mind. Throughout the remaining chapters, the concept of awareness will become a repetitive theme. This is done on purpose, because awareness alone can make all the difference in how successful we will be with our quest. Finding our moxie and having awareness, we can achieve it all.

Mind Morph

The first time I saw this comic, I chuckled and my first response to the question the guy asks was, "of course not", but then I stopped and pondered the question further. I certainly have traits that I view as negative in myself, but if I am being 100% honest, those traits do benefit me in certain situations, so at those points in time, I am glad I possess these certain characteristics.

I know a young man that is a master of persuasion. If a person has a differing opinion on a topic, he is relentless in his need to bring that person around to his way of thinking. Many of his classmates hate to be around him and avoid him in social situations. On the other hand, he is on the debate team at his high school and he is a major factor for this team winning week after week. See what I mean? In a social situation his persuasion is annoying and irritating, but on the debate team, it is most useful and beneficial. The issue that plagues this young man is not that his power of persuasion is a negative trait; it is his lack of awareness of how this trait affects his behavior and how this behavior is perceived differently in various situations. It is a matter of understanding the purpose and usefulness of a trait or behavior and using it in the best way, for the best purpose, and for the best outcome. If we work off of this thought process then there are no good or bad qualities; it is only how we use them that matters. Wow! I don't know about you, but I feel better about myself already.

Success in school, work and in life is more about the behaviors we display rather than the traits we entail. If our persuasive young man recognized that the behavior he exhibited with his classmates during social interactions was perceived as negative, and he adjusted his behavior by choosing not to engage in persuasion during this time, he has entered into the world of *mind-morph*. Mind-Morph is the ability to see into our mind objectively to identify our current thoughts, feelings, behaviors, and the morph them to meet our desired outcomes or goals. It requires looking at what we really want and behaving in a way that is beneficial to getting us what we want. This is more advantageous to our needs, than justifying those knee jerk reactions that are driven by uncontrolled emotions and unconscious habits. Instead of reacting, we can act. We can make a conscious choice to plan our action. We put this plan in place to change what we exhibit by identifying our ultimate goals, and making choices that lead us in that direction.

Positive change is not just about thinking positively. Awareness of the mind and how to direct thoughts, beliefs and emotions, opens new avenues of possibility. Our life becomes immensely different when we are the one directing our minds instead of allowing it to direct us. The power to change our life and create happiness resides with our personal self. We have the power. We just do not always embrace awareness. No one else can change what we believe and what we express as an individual. When we express love, acceptance, and respect, we create pleasant emotions within ourselves. When we express judgment, fear, jealousy, and anger we experience emotional chaos. The challenge is to master our emotional expression by being aware of our thoughts and feelings as often as possible. We are the only one who can determine the thoughts we think, the words that come out of our mouth, the emotions we create, and the behaviors we exhibit. We all have this incredible ability to talk ourselves in or out of anything. We choose our attitude and what we express is of our personal choice. We create our own weather. We can walk around creating a path of destruction from the harsh wind and rain we are spurting out or we can shine rays of sunshine while butterflies dance and birds sing in the background. Yes, this idea is a little corny, but think about how true this is. If we display a high level of self-awareness, in spite of what we are feeling or thinking, we can decide to be the tornado; cloudy, gloomy and stormy or the sun; bright, cheerful and enlightening.

What is our weather really like? Do we lose our temper quickly? Do we blame others often? Is our first emotion in most situations negative in nature? Are we more consumed about being right than being open to another's emotional state or creating a positive environment? Do we easily get defensive, blame others or ourselves, or make excuses when someone points out something about our behavior? Do we rarely apologize to others, especially those that we love? Many times the problem may be obvious to everyone but us. The culprit is our lack of self-awareness.

Time for Our Version of Reality TV

As humans we are fascinated with the wacky ways of other humans, as demonstrated in the popularity of the reality television empire. The Kardashians, American Idol, and Naked and Afraid are just a few shows that are viewed by millions every day. Since humans are well, human, people love to notice how others behave behind closed doors. With that idea of having an interview, it is time to introduce a family to assist us in our pursuit; a way to see how others handle situations by helping us learn more about ourselves.

Introducing Penelope La'Sagna. Penelope, as well as some of her family and friends, will visit us from time to time to demonstrate some important points. Penelope is a 38-year-old female. She works full-time, has a 13-year-old daughter, Penny, and has been married 15 years to her husband, Pete. Penelope is a strong, independent woman who has a giving heart and a fun spirit. We want to thank Penelope for sharing her experiences with us for the purpose of learning insight about ourselves.

As we follow along with Penelope, her family and friends, we are going to be seeing real situations. The scenarios presented are to help us gain insight to our own behavior and help us to find alternative ways to engage with others. As you continue to read, pay close attention to the influences that shape the character's behavior. If we keep in mind that all behavior is purposeful, then we recognize that there is a reason why we do what we do. There is always a reason for our actions whether we are conscious of the actual reason or not.

Our upbringing shapes us in ways we may not be aware of. We learn to modify behavior at a very young age. Our beliefs of what is right and wrong are developed, stereotypes are learned, behaviors are shaped and attitudes are formed. Over time, automatic responses are programmed through our actions and reactions. These habits are not always the most helpful to us in getting what we really want in life. Through advancements in technology we are bombarded with images, information, and messages that tell us how to be and what to think. The media can provide us with well-scripted and questionably motivated information which aides in our development of a uniformed perception of the world, at times. The information provided by the media can not only change our opinion of what we think and how we should act, but it can impact our emotions.

The people around us can be positive or negative, which can affect our response to them and our environment. Family, friends, co-workers, parents of our child's soccer team, and even the cashier at the local store, impact us daily. Societal norms shape what people expect or tolerate from one another. They give us a framework of what is acceptable and what is not acceptable in society. This concept will be discussed further in the next chapter.

Our personality shapes who we are, where our strengths lie, what areas need improvement, where we get our energy and so much more. Different personality types interact well with one another, while other types are like mixing oil and water. If there is not an understanding about how to handle the differences between individuals, problems can arise.

ACTIVITY

INFLUENCES

Circle all the things that you think influence you the most:

PEOPLE	MEDIA	PERSONAL CHARACTERISTICS
Family	Television	Outgoing
Friends	Computer	Shy
Co-Workers	Newspaper	Quiet
Acquaintences	Magazine	Talkative
Strangers	Facebook	Detailed
Service Workers	Twitter	Creative
_____	_____	_____
_____	_____	_____

As you can quickly see, MANY things influence us. Unless we really have a grasp on our self-awareness, any changes presented can create negative outcomes.

Scenario

Penelope

Sabrina

Penelope meets someone new named Sabrina. Penelope hits it off with her, and instantly feels that the two of them are already best friends. Penelope wants to hang out again, and hounds her new acquaintance with requests to meet for lunch. Finally, Sabrina agrees to hang out, and suggests that they ask another mutual friend, Katie, to go along, too. Penelope immediately tells her no and starts gossiping about Katie. Sabrina is put off by Penelope's comments, cancels the lunch date, and tells Penelope not to contact her again. Penelope is shocked at Sabrina's response, wonders what her problem is, and hangs up in anger.

Life is like Photography. We develop from the negatives."

What is missing in this scenario? Penelope's self-awareness; she is not looking at her own behavior, when she questions why Sabrina does not want to hang out anymore. Penelope is not aware that when she is gossiping about Katie, she is giving Sabrina a negative perception of who she is, and since Sabrina has just met Penelope, she makes a decision that she does not want to have a friendship with someone who gossips about her friends.

Penelope needs to consider her own thoughts, feelings and behaviors before she can have a realistic view of this situation. Penelope needs to recognize that she was gossiping about her friend, Katie, but a deeper question is, why did Penelope feel the need to gossip about Katie in the first place? What emotion was the driving force behind this gossiping behavior? When we are self-aware, we can reflect objectively to get an honest view of what occurred. When Penelope reflected factually, she identified that she really liked Sabrina and really wanted them to be close friends. Penelope loves Katie, but Katie has a personality that everyone is drawn towards, and she felt threatened when Sabrina suggested Katie join the lunch date. Penelope felt there would be little chance for her to build a strong friendship with Sabrina if Katie were there. Penelope's choice to gossip about Katie was not deliberate; it was simply a quick response to stop the idea of Katie joining them for lunch. Penelope did not intend to make Katie look bad in Sabrina's eyes, and she definitely never wanted Sabrina to view herself as malicious. Penelope learned from this situation, and realizes that if she had been in a high state of self-awareness, she would have quickly identified her emotions in the present state and would have made a choice to respond differently to Sabrina's request. Ultimately, Penelope understood the importance of being in tune to her thoughts and feelings as often as she can throughout the day.

If we have emotional reactions, such as anger or frustration, with self awareness we will start to notice many of the thoughts and small triggers that build up prior to expressing these emotions. With practice we start identifying these triggers and thoughts, which can change the interpretations in our mind. With this heightened awareness we can make better choices in our thought process long before an emotional reaction or destructive behavior takes place. It is our blind spot or narrow perspective that prevents us from seeing beyond the boundaries of our reactions and behaviors.

Managing oneself is easy to say, but as we all know, harder to do. Making changes is much easier when caught early, before the momentum of a thought and an emotion has gathered steam. These changes become simple when self-awareness is recognized sooner than later.

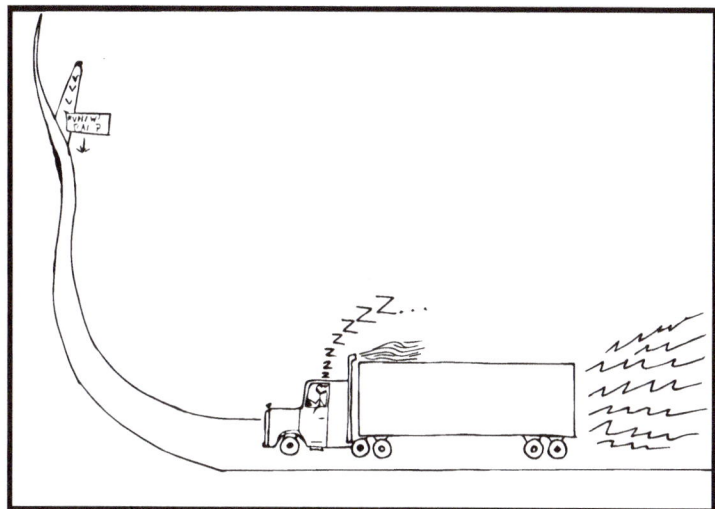

Truck going full speed while driver is asleep at the wheel. Two paths are ahead; a straight path that trucker is on & "out of control" truck ramp that will help the truck come to a stop without hurting anyone. However, trucker has to be aware to turn the truck in the direction of the ramp to safety.

Why Develop Self-Awareness?

Self-awareness is the first step in creating what we want and mastering our goals. Where we focus on our attention, our emotions, reactions, personality and behavior, we determine our direction in life. We can see where our thoughts and emotions are taking us. If we don't like where we are going, we can make changes and head in another direction. Without consciousness, making changes in our life's direction is difficult.

Self-Awareness is the key to positive change and lasting happiness. We cannot expect to change what we have not acknowledged. It provides the clarity to choose our emotions wisely, and the ability to catch our self in that moment prior to saying something destructive or thinking and believing a negative thought. Self-awareness is the means to identify our unconscious patterns and raise them in our conscious mind so these patterns can be changed for the better. It is through self-awareness that we identify and change the underlying beliefs, habits, and emotions that drive destructive behaviors.

When we no longer live by the negative thoughts in our mind, we no longer have unnecessary emotional reactions. We can get off the emotional roller coaster that has taken us for a ride. With practice we choose in a specific moment not to believe what our mind is saying. This allows us to see the emotional roller coaster coming. We can then step back from it and watch it go by without getting on. At this point we are no longer a victim to the emotions that try to control us. Once we realize we are on the "crazy coaster",

we can decide to get off at any time. No need to continually ride the ups and downs of emotions without a clear destination. The "happy train" is moving too, but along the way it has many destinations to choose from on this well-designed journey.

The Art of Becoming Self-Aware

Knowing yourself is the beginning of all wisdom." –Aristotle

The first step to self-awareness is to look at past issues we have had with others and be honest with our self. Sometimes it is so hard to believe that we messed up, that we do not allow ourselves to reflect on our actions that helped cause or prolong an argument. Admitting our part in how people react to us and treat us is a hard concept to embrace at first. Like I always tell my children, "it takes two people to have a fight." We have to look at the part we played in any problem with another person, and take responsibility for our own actions.

"They are being mean to me for no reason."

"What's wrong with Sabrina?"

"Our friendship ended and I have no idea why."

"Suddenly Sabrina is not talking to me. She just must be moody."

Take these types of personal thoughts as a warning sign. When we think this way, STOP and turn the focus back to ourselves. See if there was anything we did to push someone's buttons, start an argument, or escalate the level of disagreement. If someone blows up at us and we feel it's "out of the blue," take a moment and see if perhaps we were pushing them toward anger or resentment prior to their negative actions. Sometimes subtle nagging or condescension builds, and a friend who has put up with our negative qualities prior will suddenly not stand for it any longer. This is a good time to reflect on our actions.

When we do have an argument, listen closely to what others are saying. It can be really hard to hear negative things about our actions, but if a friend is hurt, we may have done something without even realizing it. Ask them to share their frustrations so we can learn. Self-awareness is important in our relationships. Understanding how to use it properly can be very beneficial. Self Awareness is vital to determine how our actions affect our relationships, and the point is not to act as a martyr or take the blame for everything that goes wrong in a relationship, but to understand our part so that we can choose to make changes to maintain a harmonious social life.

Be Open...Plain and Simple

READY TO MAKE A CHANGE?

Improving requires commitment and effort. Self-Awareness is developed through practice in focusing our attention on the details of our personality and behavior. Think of learning to be mindful and self aware as learning to dance. When learning to dance we have to pay attention to how and where our feet move, the motion of our hands and body, observe our partner, hear the music, recognize the beat, comprehend the floor space, and be sensitive of the other dancers. To do it right, we must be aware of all that is going on inside ourselves, as well as what is going on around us.

ACTIVITY

Self-Awareness Inventory

On a piece of paper, answer the following questions that provide a summary of a your personal self to formulate a deeper level of self-awareness.

- S - Strengths; List at least 10
- U - Understanding of core values, likes and dislikes
- M - Motivations; reflect on inspirations and enthusiasms
- M - Mannerisms; list of habits
- A - Ask for honest feedback from those you trust
- R - Relevancy of occurrences currently in your life
- Y - Ying & Yang; positive and negative that influence your destiny

"The curious paradox is that when I accept myself just as I am, then I can change."
– Carl. R. Rogers

Focus Grasshopper

In the movie, *Kung Fu Panda*, the Buddha says, " The past is history. The future is a mystery. Being present is a gift." One of our first steps in our transformation to being a more aware individual is to be more present; have consciousness. Don't fret about the past since we can't change it, and don't worry about the future since we aren't there yet. Take note of the present, becoming more self-aware and mindful of the world around us: the sights, sounds, smells, and more. Learn to observe and be a witness to every act we do and every thought that passes through our mind. Watch every desire that bubbles up inside. Observe even seemingly little things like our gestures, and the way we walk, talk, breathe, and eat. Everything can be a clue. The more watchful that we become, the internal negative chatter will occur less and less. Our thoughts become more manageable and we gain a new clarity. A clear mind is a happy mind.

We must learn to continually bring our self to the present. When we catch ourselves living in the past or imagining the future, come back to the present moment. We should not feel bad when we realize we are not in the present, this is just an old habit we need to break and replace with our new habit of being in the present. Learn to be a passive witness and observe without judgment.

Simple Ways to Improve Your Life

There is a big difference between letting life happen and consciously choosing what we think and do. We can live happy, meaningful, and fulfilling lives at any time by deciding that we are going to do it. Here are some action steps to assist in taking steps down that road to an improved way of being.

1. Notice the words that come out of other people's mouths. Do they give us energy or suck the life out of us?
2. Stop…notice the thought before it comes out of our mouths. Is this a thought that is helpful to us?
3. Notice the words that come out of our mouths. Are they purposeful and presented in a positive way?
4. Think…"We can't control others, so what can we do to make ourselves feel better?"
5. When self-criticizing occurs, quickly state 3 things we like about ourselves.
6. When we have any strong emotion, curiously ask why?
7. Is what we are doing valuable or helpful to others? If so, keep doing that. If not, ask someone how we can help them.
8. When we do take an action that we said we wanted to do…notice it!
9. Laugh every day. Fake it, if necessary.
10. Ask: "Have I done my best?" If yes, smile. If no, start now.

Yesterday is history. Tomorrow is a mystery. Today is a gift." – Bill Keane

Making recognition part of our daily routine is not hard, but like breaking a bad habit, you will have to do it consistently to see a difference. I don't know about you, but I know that I would like to exercise every day. I even have the treadmill sitting in the middle of my bedroom floor, but a lot of the times, it becomes a clothes hanger. My point is that changing anything is easier said than done. So Practice, Practice, Practice and create a positive habit. 21 days, here I come!

> Set your alarm on your smart phone and check into your emotions, thoughts, and behaviors every few hours. Stop and take a few seconds to take notice of how you are feeling, how your body is positioned and what thoughts are going through your head. Why you are feeling and thinking the way you are. Adjust to be more in line with one of your 5 emotions identified in your Cinque.

Personal Journals

This journey we are embarking on will be like a river flowing along the land. There will be times when we will be rolling along fine at a consistent, steady pace, but then we may reach a fork in the road or hit a rapid that starts to take us in a different direction in which we may not want to go. Daily writing is a great way to help us deal with the ebbs and flows that will come along the way. Having a bad day? Write about it, get it out, release it and gain understanding so that we can keep this from happening again. Have a wonderful day? Write about it. Relish in our successes, our happiness, and our joys. Experience this wonderful day all over again and recognize that we deserve it.

Studies show that when individuals write in a journal they have less stress, improved social behavior, better physical health, improved mood and affect just to name a few. Expressive writing has wonderful long-term effects and provides a way to reflect back on those things in our life that have meaning. Because a journal represents our inner most thoughts and feelings, try not to only write about the negative. Yes, it is good to release those thoughts and feelings to create opportunity for change or assist in the need for closure. Create a gratitude journal to focus on the positives in life, the things we really want and the things that we are glad to have in our life. Even though we might want things to be different, we are able to be appreciative of the things we do currently have in our life, such as, a roof over our head or food to eat. We can write down something that we are grateful for in our day or in life. By writing about gratitude, we are training our brain to think in positive terms, and giving our brain the nourishment that it needs to create happiness. And really isn't that what defines a great day?

> "Remember today for it is the beginning. Today marks the start of a brave new future."

ACTIVITY

Journal Writing For Awareness

Tips to write an effective journal.

1. Journal at the same time each day.
2. Determine a minimum amount of time you can journal each day.
3. Decide what you will use to journal. Paper and pen, computer, tablet, phone, etc
4. Establish a journaling area where you can write uninterrupted. Take a deep breath, or several, before you begin journaling. Notice your breathing throughout your writing
5. Record the date for each journal entry, and then write spontaneously as the thoughts enter your mind. Record your thoughts without editing or filtering.
6. Read your Commitment Statement.
7. Congratulate yourself for doing what you committed to do.

Commitment Statement:

I will journal everyday at_____am/pm. I will spend at least ____minutes journaling each day. I will use_____ to record my journals. My journaling location will be_____ _____ and if that is not available to me at that time then I will _____ _____. I will take ___deep breaths prior to starting my journaling, and I will notice how I feel. I will repeat this as needed. I will record the date and then start writing whatever is on my mind without criticism. I will notice that I do what I say I'm going to do.

Avoid the Funnel Cloud

It is not effortless to always be in a heightened state of awareness. It takes practice and we are not self-aware 100% of the time. No one is aware every second of every day, no matter how much we practice. Individuals are constantly moving in and out of awareness at different degrees. Think of self-awareness as a spiral similar to a funnel cloud. At different points in time we will move up and down in the awareness spiral. Sometimes it will be easier to jump out of the storm because we are more grounded and closer to land, and other times, it is more difficult, as we are caught deeper in the storm and pulled further up inside the spiraling tornado. Catching escalating behavior early makes all the difference between a small windstorm and a destructive tornado from occurring, and having a heightened level of self-awareness is key. If we use tools like self-awareness to handle the funnel cloud, we can minimize the number of large storms that appear in our life. By minimizing the number of larger storms that occur, we will not be blown off our course.

How to Handle the Funnel Cloud

Step 1: Start to Pay Attention to Frustrations.

Self-awareness breakthroughs are triggered by a sense of frustration in certain aspects of life because things aren't going the way we want them to. And while this can be frustrating, the feeling can actually start to bring a conscious awareness to a subconscious tendency that might be hindering us. This can actually be very challenging and require several big smacks upside the head before we take notice. But eventually, the dissatisfaction we may feel about a certain part of our lives slowly becomes something we can articulate. And once we can name it, we can address it.

Step 2: Start to Look for Patterns.

Now that we are good and irritated, it would be really tempting to blame the world for our tribulations. Many do just this, but in doing so, these individuals are putting the focus of control for their lives outside of themselves. They might feel better about themselves in the short run, but over the long haul, they will feel lousy because nothing will change for the better. Instead of pointing fingers at others, it's time for us to put our foot down and break the negative pattern once and for all.

Step 3: Start Asking for Input

Hopefully our frustration leads us to try to identify behavior or thought patterns that might be causing issues. Now we need to put our ego aside and see if someone else can fill in the gaps. Receiving honest feedback is not always fun, but it provides specific details that should be heard.

Step 4: Don't Despair.

It's not easy to come to unflattering realizations about ourselves and when we do, sometimes it feels like a punch in the stomach and we have to take time to recover. Even if it's something seemingly minor, it's still uncomfortable to own our imperfections. So when a new realization has been brought to our attention, this can be a hard pill to swallow. We need to fight the urge to avoid with naps, snacks, and wallowing. Don't allow the bigger the weakness to turn into a bigger bowl of ice cream. Move forward and release it, for this is now the past.

Step 5: Resolve to Do Better.

So, now we have come to terms with this recently identified area in need of development. Frequently, we are even excited to get to work, and things move forward until the next time our thoughts, behaviors, and emotions give us something more to contemplate. See if we can follow the thread of the frustration all the way through the process of becoming more self-aware.

> Keep it real. Continually be honest with yourself.

ACTIVITY

Getting to Know Yourself

Stop and take a few minutes for this activity, and be extremely honest with your answers. You will not be sharing the answers with anyone, so go lock yourself in the bathroom, go to a private spot in your yard, or truck out to the middle of nowhere if you need to. Just be in a place that you can reflect and feel comfortable to honestly answer the questions. This is a rare opportunity to reflect about yourself with no judgment expressed by what you write.

- What's your passion?
- What would you do in life if you did not need to work for money?
- Where do you want to be in 5, 10, 20 or 40 years?
- What are your fundamental life values? What are you grateful for?
- Who are the 3 most important people in your life?
- What is your biggest dream? What will you choose to sacrifice for your dream to come true?
- What are the 3 things in your life that you would like to change?
- When was the last time you laughed out loud?
- Do you like your birthdays?
- When was the last time you tried something new?
- When was the last time you did something spontaneously?
- Which are the most memorable moments from your past?
- Forget your real age for a second – now tell yourself how old are you?
- How important is social approval for you? Do you live for others or for yourself?
- What was the last life lesson you learned?
- When was the last time you helped someone? Did you ever help a complete stranger?
- What is your greatest fear? Is the cup half empty or half full for you?
- Which word describes your personality best?
- What inspires you? When was the last time you cried?
- What was the biggest change initiated by you in the past 5 years?
- What's your life's biggest achievement?
- When was the last time you were proud of yourself?
- If everything were possible where would you live?
- What stops you from making the first step towards your dream?
- When was the last time you took risk?
- Who are the 3 people who had most powerful influence on you?
- What is happiness for you? Are you at peace with yourself?
- What habits would you like to quit? Why don't you start today?
- How much are you ready to sacrifice for successful career?
- What you will never forget? Usually do you listen to your heart or to your brain?
- Which were the most emotional moments of your life?
- What are the most colorful, vivid, strong, impressive periods of your life?
- How many times have you fallen in love? How many times has your heart been broken?
- What keeps you motivated to carry on?
- Do you know how it feels to wake up with a smile?
- If not for financial matters, would you work where you are working now?
- How much time do you spend on social networks?

Make time to answer the questions in the previous activity. From answering these questions, I was amazed at what I "learned" about myself. Well, not actually learned, more like confessed and was willing to admit. By acknowledging this information, I now have a better understanding of the areas where I need to start my quest. Through acceptance, I have embraced self-awareness, and I am taking responsibility for my thoughts, feelings and behaviors, especially those that have lead to my own self-sabotage in the past. Once I take responsibility for my actions, the result is a conscious choice to make the needed changes and control the direction of my interaction, and my life.

FYI, my three words are determined, independent and lively.

Social Awareness

Social Awareness is the walls of a house. The walls combined with the foundation create support for the roof. It plays a fundamental part of a house's structure and repairs must be made when cracks are visible to keep the walls from crumbling.

Gritty Lasagna: The Print in Blueprint

SOCIAL AWARENESS

As I began writing this chapter, I was trying to think of a simple, concise way to describe social awareness. Then it hit me...Walt Disney World. I love Walt Disney World, and spend quite a bit of time there with my family. As I reflect on those trips, there is one example that occurs every single time I am in the parks. It is a quick, but yet, powerful instance of someone who lacks social awareness. No, you don't need to have been to Disney World to understand my story, believe me you will quickly realize my point.

Every night there is a fireworks display that occurs inside the Magic Kingdom Park. It is a beautiful display that appears over the castle, the centerpiece of the park, and some of the best views come from standing on Main Street, USA. This is the walkway between the castle and the entrance and exit to the park, which is another reason for standing at this location. If you are leaving the park right after the firework finale, this is the best place to stand to gain quick access to the exit gates.

So, we gather with thousands of other park attendees on Main Street, USA, watching this beautiful fireworks display. Once the show is over, the majority of the guests will turn around 180 degrees and head in the opposite direction for the exit to the park. This is a mass exodus, where wall-to-wall people are taking synchronized steps with those around them to get to the same final destination. And then it happens, the person in front of you comes to an abrupt stop to bend down and tie their shoe, or whatever they feel they must do at that exact moment in time, and you go slamming into them, and then the chain reaction begins. People from behind, start bumping into the person in front of them, and so on and so on. No, it's not an awful thing, but it shows how unaware someone can be about their actions and how those actions will affect others. I am always amazed at how an individual can be surrounded by this extremely large group migrating in the same direction and not recognize that their sudden stop will affect those behind them. The scary thought...it happens every time I am there, and this reinforces my belief that there is a sea full of socially unaware people swimming around me everyday. Social Awareness is about paying attention to the world around us and understanding our impact on that world. Basically, we need to have a clue that our actions have a ripple affect.

Although I am frustrated and angry at this person's low level of social awareness, I must work hard to not react negatively. Especially when exhausted from a long day in the park, this can be challenging. I have to be aware of my reaction to their behavior, as this reaction, too, impacts those around me. If I allow the venomous emotions I am feeling to show externally, I can make this situation much worse. Without self-awareness and social awareness, I allow negative thinking to control my emotions and behaviors, and my actions will ultimately impact my family, tainting a wonderful day due to an inconsequential moment that in the grand scheme of life, really doesn't matter. I must make a choice to act instead of react.

Be responsible for the energy you bring into the world" - Anonymous

Decide where to Stand

Do we want to stand in or outside the box? We need to be aware of our current location and then decide what view we want to have in life. Individuals can work towards building a higher level of social awareness every day. By knowing what is socially acceptable and acting accordingly, we have the ability to understand and respond to the needs of others. Awareness of social situations is about carefully considering what people expect and want then planning to communicate with them in a way that is intended to meet that need, as well as our own. In addition, it allows us to understand other people, and how they perceive us, such as our attitudes and our responses to them in the moment.

Higher social awareness means having a solid understanding about who we are and how we relate to the world around us. It is realizing that it's not all about us. When we have social awareness, we are able to consider others, observe their emotions, and notice their actions and reactions. We are able to ask questions, listen, and learn what other people are feeling. We are able to understand their perspective and determine what factors influenced them for the good or the bad. Even though their perspective and their experiences might be quite different than ours, we can put ourselves in their shoes and understand their feelings, needs and concerns.

We can ask ourselves if we are in tune with other people's wants and needs. Are we curious about why people do what they do? Or do we find ourselves thinking, "who cares why did they do it, it's annoying so they should stop." It is typical to get caught in our box because it is our perspective. It is more difficult to get outside of our box. When we stand on the outside of our box, we have a whole different view and our perspective grows. If it were easy then everyone would stand outside of their box.

Tide Factors

Ever really thought about how we became the individual we are? When I ask most people this, their first response is, "my parents". Yes, they are correct, but it is so much farther reaching, as everything and everyone shape who we are. Any experience in our life makes an impression and plays a part in shaping whom we are. This is one of the awe-ha moments for many.

Many factors are to blame for who we have become. Just joking, but only about the blame part. No one and nothing is to blame for our negative traits. If we look at our past in a positive, mindful state we can find the value in all of our experiences. We, alone, are the architects of our life, but by understanding how our experiences form our thoughts, we can take beneficial action to make sure we control the design.

The saddest aspect of life right now is that science gathers knowledge faster than society gathers wisdom." – Isaac Asimov

We are complex beings and the evidence of that complexity is far reaching. Think about it. Even with identical twins born to the same parents, unless they live in a bubble and have the exact same occurrences throughout their entire life, they will be different in many ways, and those differences are based on their exposure to a large variety of factors. These types of factors that shape us are broken down into basic categories.

- **Environmental** factors are characteristics of our broader environment such as economic conditions, social and cultural norms, and political factors that affect our individual behavior.

- **Social** factors includes relationships with family, friends, co-workers, supervisors and subordinates, as well as memberships in groups such as unions, sororities, and fraternities. The behavior of others is also part of our social environment. Even the norms, rules, laws or reward systems that we are exposed to form our social experiences.

- **Personal** factors include physical and personal attributes like age, sex, race, and education. Something as simple as the contour of a nose or the resemblance to someone shapes us.

- **Psychological** factors are less observable characteristics and attributes such as values, attitudes, personality and aptitudes that affect behavior.

- **Physiological** factors include how we feel; like being tired and or hungry, having racing thoughts, hot flashes, physical pain, and the array of human emotions we experience daily.

All of these factors are equally important and are always constantly at work influencing our emotions and actions. We have an internal monitor gauging our feelings, and when we choose to watch the monitor we know when one or many of these factors are pulling us off our desired path. When we acknowledge our feelings, we can then intervene at low tide, with stable calm water, instead of waiting until the water gets over our heads and we start violently crashing into the sand. In other words, we start clashing with other people. Awareness of our self can be a calming social factor for others. Ultimately, it's our choice to battle or empathize with other people and their life situations that determines the outcomes of our interactions.

I Feel Ya

Empathy is the action of understanding, being aware of, being sensitive to, and vicariously experiencing the feelings, thoughts, and experience of another. Empathizing with someone is to understand an individual's point of view. It doesn't mean we have to agree with their point of view, it just means that we can consider what they are feeling and why they are feeling that way.

When we are empathetic we acknowledge the emotions of others, are thoughtful and considerate of their feelings, and make decisions with regards to our interaction with them, we take their feelings into consideration. But empathy is not sympathy, which is acknowledging another person's emotional hardships and providing comfort to them. Many people think if they are empathetic that they are soft and have to give in to the needs of others. This could not be further from the truth. We may get angry with our child and snap at them because it is frustrating that we constantly have to tell them to clean their room. In this moment we are not as self-aware as we could be, so this occurs. The child gets very upset. Quickly we are dealing with the fact that we snapped at them instead of dealing with the issue at hand… the dirty bedroom. If we are empathetic, we can clearly see why they are upset. Snapping did occur, and when we put ourselves in their shoes, we can understand that it is not fun to be yelled at and why they would prefer to be spoken to about the issue in a calm manner. Although, we need to deal with our negative behavior that escalated this situation, we can stand firm on the position; The bedroom needs to be clean and stay clean, as we pass out consequences for not following through with their assigned chores. We can appreciate that this negative way of expressing the frustration over the dirty bedroom was unnecessary and a more positive way of expressing our emotions should be explored for the future. Having a higher level of social awareness and self-awareness, we apologize to them for how we handled ourselves, but we can make it clear that the expectation that the chores are done daily has not changed.

Empathy can really make a difference between having a happy, loving home or a house were people just co-exist. Based on the situation with the dirty bedroom, the next time we have a similar issue, we can be more self-aware of how we are feeling at the time, and think through our interaction with our child and consider how they will feel based on our choice of action. By trying to understand how our child will perceive our communication choice, we can figure out the best way to approach the problem. One thing to remember, one size does not fit all. We may need to approach the same issue in two very different approaches for different individuals. The idea is to elicit the best response from each person. Knowing our audience helps us to be successful in gauging another's reaction. When we don't know an individual personally, we should just use common courtesy; treat others how you would like to be treated. You cannot go wrong with that philosophy, as we all want to be treated with respect. Empathy is our most valuable resource for conflict resolution and developing a higher level of social awareness.

My parents told me when I was little, I would cry when my sister got into trouble. Guess that's why I am the social worker and she is the attorney.

Being aware of how our actions impact others will help us make wiser decisions, become more likable to others, increase the positivity in our relationships and will boost our own self-confidence. The awareness of how our actions impact others will create a climate of happiness and guide us to living a more satisfying life.

Those with empathetic skills:
- Are stable and calm
- Are understanding of others
- Embrace personal responsibility
- Help others effectively problem solve
- Admit wrong doings and move on
- Feel grateful for what they do have
- Are concerned about how their actions affect others
- Accept responsibility for their behavior
- Don't need others to intervene to avoid personal destruction
- Have control over their emotions and actions

Those without empathetic skills:
- Inclined to be in a state of emotional distress
- Are very judgmental of others
- Embrace the ability to bully or control others
- Negatively manipulate or con to take advantage of others
- Lack remorse, shame or guilt
- Feel overly-entitled
- Fell unconcerned about wreaking havoc in the lives of others
- Do not accept blame
- May end up finding themselves in trouble with the law
- May suffer from mental health issues

If we lack empathy, we are not inhuman, as it may not be an intention to make others feel bad. It could be a learned trait to protect ourselves from past situations or maybe just the fact that we are getting older. Studies show that we develop more selfishness as we age. It is only through making a conscious choice to change for a different result that we learn to be more kind, compassionate, and selfless.

Quick Empathy Building Tips

- Stand in the other individual's shoes and view the world from his or her perspective
- Try to comprehend the pressures, obligations, expectations, and demands placed upon this individual
- If an individual voices themselves inappropriately or they are rambling on, making confusing statements, ask them to clarify what the problem is or what they mean
- Consider the thinking behind their opinion or argument

OUR PERCEPTION BECOMES OUR REALITY

Ever receive an email that is written in all capital letters? What is the first thing that comes to mind? Generally, the first thought is the sender is upset with us for some reason and they may be yelling in a written form. So we form an opinion based on our perceptions and beliefs. Our perception becomes our reality and quickly our mood changes. We start to feel angry, upset or even anxious. So what do we do next? I bet someone immediately typed an angry email and sent it to the sender, only to find out later that when the sender sent the original email, they had the cap lock button on. There was nothing more to it. We end up feeling embarrassed and have created a negative situation with the sender based on a reason that never existed. If we have a higher level of self-awareness, we would be able to view this situation in a more objective way. We would not react, but act. Perceptions and beliefs are powerful and unless something is offered to shake our inner truth, they will shape our attitude.

Perceptions and beliefs are housed in our minds and are not actions. The basis to our way of thinking is a belief. We do not question beliefs, they are our truths, and we take them for what they are. Values are an example of a belief, our foundational way of thinking. Perception is the method or technique used in thinking. It is our point of view. Perceptions are the input filter for what we see and hear, and are formed based on our belief and in return influence our attitudes. Our attitude is the outward actions of our internal perceptions and beliefs; it is the performance of our thinking. Our attitudes are directly influenced by our thoughts, and our thoughts are directly influenced by our perceptions, which are formed from our beliefs.

Social perception is the study of how people form impressions and make inferences about other people. To learn about other people, we rely on information from people's physical appearance, verbal communication, and nonverbal communication including facial expressions, tone of voice, gestures, body position and movement, touch, and gaze.

From these emotional expressions, we interpret what is meant, and this is our perception. These perceptions form our beliefs about other people. If nothing occurs to change our perceptions, then the belief is reinforced and becomes stronger. The stronger those beliefs, the more they seem unshakeable, and the more we will find evidence to support them. Beliefs are formed through repeated thoughts, and are based on our perceptions of many types of influencing factors. If these beliefs create a negative mindset or limit our ability to live in a manner we would like, they are considered limiting.

The first step in overcoming limiting beliefs is to identify those beliefs. Without giving a long lecture, let's present two major points we need to understand. The beliefs that we hold are either empowering or dis-empowering. It should never be a question of which belief is right versus wrong. Our mindset and our ways of thinking either help us or hold us back. Our beliefs become our reality, so we must begin thinking in terms that will help us achieve our goals.

> "Our actions of the past should not define who we are today. Our actions of today should help to define who we want to become."

Scenario

Penelope, Pete and Penny are home for the holidays. Pete is not happy about being there. He has been dreading this trip for months. You see, his big brother Terry will be home, as well, and Pete is not looking forward to spending time with his brother. Pete told Penelope, "I never really had a close relationship with Terry. Terry was always mean to me, and getting me into trouble when we were growing up." Penelope said to him, "Try not to let that bother you. You know how kids can be." When Terry finally arrives, Pete immediately feels a surge of negative emotions about Terry's presence. Unfortunately, this situation is affecting Pete's attitude for the day, and he begins to snap at his wife and children and ultimately pulls away from the family activities. Later in the day, Pete walks by a room when he overhears Terry talking positively about Pete. Terry is going on and on about Pete's strengths and Terry says how proud he is of his younger brother. Pete is stunned. He realizes that his perception of Terry for all these years was incorrect, and due to the change in his thoughts and beliefs, he realizes he no longer feels resentment towards Terry. Pete feels foolish, but walks away with a smile on his face.

Pete

Terry

Perceptions blur our visions, so if we are thinking negatively, those negative thoughts will shape our actions. Look more closely at the above scenario. For years, Pete perceived that the relationship with his brother was damaged. This perception further shaped that relationship, creating a self-fulfilling prophecy for Pete. I don't know about you, but I have many situations  similar to this where I have perceptions that have shaped my choices. What I realize now is that no matter what perceptions consume my thoughts, I lead my life by my positive guiding *Cinque*. If Pete does this, then he creates a short goal based on that driving life feeling. Pete says, "I want to be home for the holidays and feel peaceful when I see my brother. Up to this point it hasn't been working to just tell myself to not feel negatively towards Terry so I'm going to create a short-term goal to get what I do want." So consider when Pete went home for the holidays how differently his experience would be if he had gone in with this short-term goal from the beginning. It is very fortunate that Pete overheard Terry speaking positively about him or Pete would have left once again feeling negatively about his brother and his visit home. If Pete creates his short tem goals from his *Cinque*, then if nothing else, he is making choices and creating a path based on positive reasons. I don't know about you, but it is always more comfortable and peaceful for me feeling positive than not.

Pete's childhood and the incidents that he and Terry shared formed the relationship Pete chose to have with Terry. Pete realizes that his past has been shaping his perception of his sibling and more so, this past has had a huge impact on the way their relationship has been up to now. You see, Pete perceived that Terry didn't like him; therefore, Pete decided he didn't like Terry either. Because of their past relationship, Pete never put himself in a position to get close to Terry because he didn't want to be hurt by his brother. Once Terry took a different action, speaking positively about Pete's strengths, Pete had a different thought about Terry, which led Pete to a positive feeling about his brother. The moral of this story: what a person perceives as happening is more influential than what is actually occurring.

MIND CLUTTER

At any given moment there are many different thoughts that have set up camp in our brain. We are thinking about a conversation that took place over dinner last night, an argument that you witnessed between two friends or a situation that occurred with a co-worker earlier in the day. Whatever it is, these thoughts that stay in our mind generate emotions and behaviors whether we are conscious of the effects or not. By getting rid of thoughts that have no positive benefit is helpful is our overall mental health. Keep it, Trash it or Give it away, is a helpful process to use when we need to sort through our thoughts, feelings, beliefs to create change in our life. It is simple and effective. If Pete would have considered using this process on his beliefs surrounding Terry, he would have trashed his negative ideas long ago and his relationship with Terry could have significantly been altered. Even if Terry really did have negative thoughts about Pete all this time and continued having those thoughts, so what? We can't control how others think. What we do, we do for ourselves and for ourselves only. If nothing else, this would have allowed Pete to release these negative thoughts from his mind, and make room for more positive ones.

Gritty Lasagna: The Print in Blueprint

TRASH IT   KEEP IT   GIVE IT AWAY

Cleaning up our mind clutter to be in alignment with our goals changes our perceptions and beliefs. This creates a pathway in our brain to allow our actions to work toward our goal instead of away from it.

Pete has decided to "Keep" the memory of Terry saying nice things about him because that feels good to Pete. Pete wants to be more social when he is feeling good which is helpful while interacting with others. This thought will help Pete achieve his goal. Pete has decided to "Give Away" the thought that he doesn't have a close relationship with Terry. This isn't a horrible thought and it may serve someone else, but it doesn't help Pete achieve his goal because he will keep his distance, which won't magically create a close relationship with his brother. Pete also decided that he will "Trash" the idea that Terry is mean to him and all the negative emotions that go along with this thought. When it comes down to it, Pete can't prove that Terry really wants to harm him, especially since what he has overheard conflicts with this idea.

ACTIVITY

Trash it, Keep it, Give it Away.

Goal: Spend time with my family and enjoy each other's company

Keep It - currently useful and beneficial to manifesting the life imagined
Give It Away - not needed or not useful anymore, but it might benefit someone else
Trash It - validity is difficult to prove and/or not useful or beneficial in attaining the goal

Keep It	Give It Away	Trash It
Terry thinks I have a lot of strengths and is proud of me.	I don't have a close relationship with Terry.	Terry is mean to me and wants to harm me.

State a situation that clutters your mind _____
_____
_____

Social Awareness

ACTIONS CREATE REFLECTIONS

Have you looked into a mirror lately? When we look in a mirror, what do we see? We see a reflection of ourselves. Reflections are constantly coming at us from outside sources. Look around, and notice the people in our life who serve as our mirrors every day, and take on this role, inadvertently. If we pay close attention to these individuals, we are given a wonderful opportunity to see our reflection through their behaviors and by their verbal and non-verbal communication offerings. Gather that important information, because people say things to us or about us for a reason. Remember, all behavior is purposeful, and when we have a higher level of social awareness, we can acknowledge specific words spoken, facial gestures, and tone in their voice that reflect who we are at that moment. This knowledge brings us closer to truly recognizing ourselves, but only if we can recognize that our actions produce this reflection.

All of our knowledge is the offspring of our perceptions." – Leonardo Da Vinci

Scenario

Recently, when Penny was out with a group of friends, a boy she was talking to told her that she talks a lot. Penny knew she had the gift of gab, but no one had ever told her that before. She started to worry that she does talk too much, and decided she doesn't want people to think she monopolizes conversations, so she would make some changes. The next time she is out with her friends, she decides to keep her conversation to a minimum. She is hanging out with a group of friends one afternoon, and they start talking about a new place to eat this weekend. Several times throughout the conversation, Penny's friends ask her what she thinks about the idea before the weekend plans are finalized. Wanting to keep her conversations to a minimum, and not to seem overly chatty, she quickly answers the questions with words like, "OK", "Good" and "Fine", so not to be rude to her friends.

Penny

Why do you think her friends are asking Penny her thoughts? Oh, I don't know. Maybe its because Penny says nothing or answers them with one word, like "Fine", "OK", "Good." They ask her because she doesn't talk enough. They ask her because they want to involve her in the conversation and value her opinions. When Penny considers her friends as her mirror, she can see her reflection and let go of this belief that she monopolizes conversations. She will see that her friends want to hear from her and value her voice and what she has to say. Believe me, if she does start to monopolize a conversation, she will know it. The girls will tell her to be quiet, or cut her off. Teenage girls usually have no problem telling others what they don't like. They just aren't the best at hearing it when it is directed toward them. Result: DRAMA!

Create social scripts ahead of time. Write out what you might say in situations prior to meeting people, like receiving a compliment or feedback from others.

It is important to be aware how others see us in general and in specific situations. The more insight we have in this area, the less we have to worry about. It is possible to see exactly how others see us, however it takes courage. Time to take a peak in the mirror, if we dare.

Mirrors are everywhere and many times we understand the reflections, but don't want to actually acknowledge it. Consider a baby looking at itself in the mirror for the first time, they are happy at the reflection. They will smile and babble at the baby. They like what they see so they continue to look at the mirror, laughing and giggling. When we look in the mirror if we don't like what we see, what do we do? Typically, we stop looking.

If you thought that was enough, guess what else the mirror shows? Consider how important it is for another's well being if we are aware of what you put in their life. "Treat others as you would treat yourself." I personally would treat myself with love, respect and joyfulness, but I can tell you honestly that I don't always treat others that way. I fail at social competence from time to time. Social competence is your ability to understand other people's moods, behavior, and motives in order to improve the quality of your relationships.

Scenario

Penny

Penelope

Penelope and Penny have a pretty good relationship. Well, as well as a relationship can be between a mother and her teenage daughter. Penelope worries about Penny, as mothers tend to do. So when Penny wants to cut off her beautiful, long curly hair, to a punk hairstyle, Penelope tells her no. Penelope thinks she is silly to want to cut off her hair. She can't understand why someone would want to cut something so beautiful. Also, as a mom she is concerned about how people will perceive Penny with this type of hairstyle, and what people will think of her as a mother to allow this to occur. Penelope doesn't want the classmates at school and others to tease her or think negatively of her. Penny is very upset, and continues to plead with her mom to treat her like a young adult and trust her decisions. This battle goes on for quite some time, until Penelope finally sees the reflection. She realizes that she is making her decision based on her own negative experience when she cut her hair as a youth, and is projecting her concerns and biases onto her daughter. When she sees the reflection, she realizes that this is not want she wants to be placing onto Penny's shoulders. She wants Penny to be a strong, independent woman who is confident no matter what. "What's the big deal," Penelope finally asks? "It's hair. It will grow back. If this haircut doesn't work out, she can try something new."

The hairstyle is not permanent, but the impact of Penelope making decisions for her daughter and projecting her own biases onto Penny will have a lingering effect. If Penelope interferes with all of Penny's decisions without considering the result, do you think that Penny will end up being a strong, independent, confident young woman? My guess is no.

Seeing how our actions affect others will assist us in recognizing other's perceptions of our actions. If we are not effective at this we may have an emotional dependency, which comes out of our need to be right or our need for approval or both. So who cares if we are right? Did I hear you say, "Well, I Care"! I used to say the same thing. I had such a strong need to be correct, and did not understand what was wrong with that thinking. Over time I realized that being right is irrelevant. This necessity is a limiting belief and typically leads to an exhibition of behaviors not in alignment with my goals. Who cares if we are right if the fight to prove ourselves stops us from making progress towards our goals, adds to our stress level, and impacts others around us negatively. We should strive to take a different path towards being emotionally self-sufficient and responsible for our actions by changing our thinking of the situation. Our beliefs become our reality. In the bigger picture, we should be more concerned with reaching our goals and ask ourselves if what I am thinking, feeling, and doing is getting me closer to my reaching my goals and life's dreams. If not, then stop and adjust accordingly.

As people, we can engage in some pretty interesting behaviors. Our personal awareness is key when interacting with other people. All human behavior is purposeful, and if I continue to think that the person causing the human traffic jam on Main Street, USA is just idiotic then I have just given away all of my power to effect my juju positively. I want to be aware of my forward progress and guide myself smoothly to the exit instead of mindlessly crashing against one another. Our awareness affects others but has a lasting effect on our self because that is the person who walks in my shoes from the park to my house.

"Treat others as you should treat yourself."

Learn to examine situations from multiple angles. Change your seat when you cannot see another's perspective.

EMOTIONAL INTELLIGENCE

Emotional Intelligence is the roof of a house. The roof protects your house from the elements. If the roof is damaged it allows the appliances and furnishings in our house to be damaged by exposing them to the elements.

EMOTIONAL INTELLIGENCE

Chapter 5

I think we can all think of times our emotions pulled us off our path to what we were really trying to achieve. Instead of being a slave to our emotions, we can use them to keep us on our path because it all starts with awareness. One day while I was working at home, I found myself being called by the leftover cupcakes from my son's birthday party. I will recount what went on in my head and the actions I took to manage my emotions.

I feel stressed because I want the cupcake in my kitchen? Of course, I didn't say it that way. I plainly said in my head, "I want the cupcake in the kitchen." I didn't identify any stress. Why would I be stressed about a cupcake? That's just silly! Or is it?

Through awareness I recognize that I'm having a spontaneous want...a cupcake, and then I'm aware that the cupcake is not in alignment with my truly desired goal, which is to lose weight. I'm now aware of the misalignment of the spontaneous want and the desired goal. Great, so I just won't eat the cupcake! I'm now aware that I'm not even hungry. "This is easy breezy", runs through my head. I continue on with my work for thirty-two seconds until the next powerful wave comes over me. "I WANT a cupcake!" pops back with a vengeance. Didn't I just address this issue? Right, the cupcake won't help me lose weight. Fifteen seconds later, really the cupcake again! I take a deep breath and carry on. Four seconds later, okay, I'm going to take a look to see if I can find a substitute for the cupcake. I open the pantry and see Oreos, Chips Ahoy, Reese's Miniatures, Goober's, M&M's, so I quickly close the door and think, "what the hell is this place, a candy store!" I then go to the refrigerator and open the doors and immediately see through the tiny window of the pullout drawer more Reese Cups and Hershey chocolate bars. I feel myself starting to break. The thought that I could just have one cupcake and be done instead of eating several fun size candy bars becomes my way to rationalize my thinking. I stop myself and think NO, stepping away from the now closed doors of my refrigerator. I look at the cupcake; I reach for the cupcake; I run away from the cupcake and return to my chair. I'm aware that this cupcake is taking my focus off my work, and I then recognize there is tightness in my neck. I can now see that I'm stressed about this stupid cupcake! I need a different focus! As I turn my head, I notice what is right outside my window, the lush trees, shimmering pond, and chirping birds. I take a deep breath and think, "people who persevere get paid off with their desired goal". I meet these people every day, and they are in varying steps on their path to their goals. I remember a few of their stories and see several of their faces. I'm now aware that I'm feeling grateful for my surroundings and for the opportunity to meet so many great people every week who are so inspiring to me and to those around them. Having gratitude for the things I do have in life helps when I feel like I have to sacrifice those spontaneous wants to get to my long-term goal that has no immediate payoff. This is how I can use my emotional intelligence to help myself through stressful moments, no matter how small the stressor may seem. I am making progress, as I am aware that in the past, I would have already eaten the cupcake and would have moved on to the candy bars, too. I took a step towards my long-term goal of losing weight, not very gracefully, but it is a step, nonetheless.

> "Your emotions are the slaves to your thoughts, and you are the slave to your emotions."
> —Elizabeth Gilbert, Eat, Pray, Love

WHAT IS EMOTIONAL INTELLIGENCE?

It has been long thought that having a high IQ is the key to success and achieving personal goals. If that is so, explain to me the various highly intelligent individuals that run around every day, but can't maintain a friendship or secure that great business deal with a needed financial institution. They are academically brilliant but socially unskilled. Recent studies show that the most successful people are not those with the highest IQ, but with the greatest EQ. EQ refers to emotional intelligence and it is the capacity to be aware of, control, and express one's emotions, and to handle interpersonal relationships judiciously and empathetically. When it comes to happiness and achieving success in life, EQ helps us build stronger personal relationships, achieve our career and personal goals, and identify our individual strengths.

Because emotional intelligence is the skill to identify, understand, use, and manage emotions in constructive ways, we are able to relieve stress, effectively communicate with others, recognize the emotional states of those around us, overcome challenges, and reduce conflict. Bottom line, EQ impacts the way we behave and the way we interact with others and the world around us.

Individuals with high emotional intelligence are able to successfully engage with others in a positive way, because of the ability to recognize their own emotional state and the emotional states of others so that they can pull people in, instead of pushing them away. This is important in both our personal and professional life. Having a higher emotional intelligence can help navigate the social complexities of our workplace, effectively lead and motivate others, and excel more easily in our career. In fact, many companies now view EQ in job candidates as important as their technical abilities needed to do the job. When dealing with others, EQ allows us to have a better understanding of how they are feeling and provides us the ability to choose the best way to communicate with them.

Those with higher emotional intelligence experience less stress because they have the ability to recognize their emotional state, and can more easily identify the cause of their stressors and choose an effective way to reduce their stress so that their emotions stay in check. This is important because uncontrolled stress greatly impacts our mental health. This can cause anxiety, depression, and mood swings which can lead to feeling lonely and isolated. These all impact our ability to form relationships with others, which in turn, adds to our stress level. This is a nasty cycle that needs to be broken.

Emotional intelligence in simplest terms is having good people skills. Some people just get along with others very well. They are great at listening, resolving problems, and know exactly what to say, and exactly how to say it, regardless of what their actual position may be. These people are good at controlling their own emotions. In the most stressful situations, they keep their cool, stay calm and sustain a positive outlook in order to get the job done. They look honestly at themselves, accept feedback and take criticism well, and in turn use this new information productively to improve themselves, their work and their relationships. With self and social awareness we can take steps to increase our emotional intelligence.

ACTIVITY

Notice Areas of High EQ

Even if we have areas in our lives that we know our EQ is low and it is pulling us off of our desired path in life, we can probably identify other areas in which we have high EQ and see success after success. Let us use our emotions as a guide to inform us if we are being pushed or pulled off our path. Awareness is the key to build our EQ which will keep us on our path to success. Think about areas in which you have the highest EQ and start building from there. Remember high EQ isn't about not having any emotions; it's about how we choose to deal with our emotions. Notice our feelings and connecting them to what we want is important. Is our current state of mind helping us get closer to what we want?

Those with high emotional intelligence:

- Successfully manage difficult situations
- Gain respect from others
- Express themselves calmly
- Lead and guide others
- Ask other people for assistance, when needed
- Stay calm under pressure
- Are aware of their emotional state to control their reactions to people or situations
- Know the best thing to say to get the best result
- Show grit and perseverance to get things done by keeping their goal in front of them
- Look to the positive even in the most difficult situations
- Pull out the useful information in a situation so that mistakes are not repeated

KNOWING WHEN TO TAKE COVER

The skills of emotional intelligence may come more naturally to some people, but these skills can be developed and strengthened over time for those who are struggling in this area. There are many ways that raising emotional intelligence can be accomplished and in doing so we can significantly reduce our stress level and be better equipped to deal with conflicts and unexpected situations. We experience unproductive emotions for many reasons. So, what are the reasons you say? Well, that is yet to be determined. The most important thing to remember is: it's not what happens that matters but how we respond that really counts. When our needs are adequately met, we feel our life has meaning and purpose. Not meeting these basic emotional needs leaves us with a feeling that life is pointless which results in a wide range of emotional disruptions. When we live in a way that meets most of our emotional needs, we enjoy greater emotional stability and achieve self-regulation. Knowing what we need in life is the first step to creating an understanding beyond our emotions and to obtaining those greater life goals. By really thinking about these needs and enacting a plan to pursue activities that are likely to help fulfill them, we gain a higher level of emotional intelligence and in the end this plan guides us to reaching our goals.

Everything we experience produces an emotional response that influences an action. Sometimes emotions move us to act before we even have a chance to think rationally about them. It's in that brief moment of action that speaks to our current level of emotional intelligence. Being able to control our emotions depends in part on how much we feed a particular emotion or give attention to that feeling. But it's more than that. Emotional intelligence requires an understanding of our personal moods, recognizing when and why we are experiencing a specific emotion, and having effective strategies in place to influence our reactions. If you ever find yourself about to be tossed around helplessly in a hysterical tornado of emotion and need some underground shelter for protection, then let's work together to get an advance meteorological report to better weather the storm.

The fallout shelter gives us space to gain awareness and control so that we don't get taken away by the emotional tornado.

To be emotionally healthy, a person needs to:

- Feel safe and secure
- Regularly receive quality attention
- Maintain a sense of influence and control over his or her life
- Feel part of a greater community
- Experience friendship, fun, love, and intimacy with significant people
- Achieve a recognizable role in life that offers a sense of competency and achievement
- Be extended but not stressed to avoid stagnation, boredom, and to enhance self-esteem and a sense of accomplishment in life

RETRAIN YOUR BRAIN

Raising our EQ is not hard, and can be learned. We start with retraining our brain. Like anything we say or do, all information is processed through our brain, which takes in information in and begins to create instinctual action. Like any negative habit we have, we need to break the pattern and engage in a new behavior that gets us closer to our desired goal. By engaging in this new positive behavior over and over, we start to retrain our brain, and before you know it, this new habit becomes involuntary. This is what we need to do to raise our emotional intelligence.

We start by being aware of our emotions, which in turn will positively affect our decision-making abilities. By controlling the emotional side of our brain, we keep our emotions in balance and control the reactions to those emotions. When we learn how to positively use both our rational and emotional brain, our memory takes notice, and over time, our memory will respond with access to a wide range of choices and an increased ability to make good decisions with our emotions staying balanced automatically. When a new event arises, our brain will involuntarily react in this new, positive way and prevent us from repeating earlier mistakes.

People wait all week for Friday, all year for summer and all life for happiness."

Scenario

Penelope

Penelope is standing in line at the grocery store and sees that the checkout cashier is very unhappy, and is moving aggressively as she scans the groceries. Penelope notices that she, herself, is feeling quite content and happy at the moment and thinks, "That woman is having a bad day." Of course Penelope knows that the cashier's attitude has nothing to do with her. A few minutes later, it's Penelope's turn to check out. The cashier has not taken any action of acknowledgment of Penelope except for the fact that she is violently stuffing Penelope's groceries into the bags. Penelope can feel her face get hot, as her blood starts to boil, just watching the cashier. Penelope asks the cashier, "Did you hear that there may be some undercover filming at this store today?" Before the cashier can respond Penelope adds, "If I had known that, I would have put on my good sweats before I left the house." Penelope laughs to herself because the thought of being caught on film in her current state would be a sight for television, but she is also feels her shoulders loosen as she is relieved because she knows her question is conversational and not factual. Penelope gives the whew sign to the cashier who then responds with a slight smile and a "yeah, really!" The cashier then looks Penelope in the eye and with concern, tells her that she will double bag her milk so the bag won't break. Penelope expresses her appreciation to the cashier and gives her a big smile and "have a great day" before she heads out the store.

Even though Penelope's blood started to boil in the grocery store, she was able to be her own observer and didn't marinate in her negative response to the cashier. How did Penelope use the following to gain control over her emotional state?

- Recognized emotions
- Reduced stress
- Noticed non-verbal signs
- De-escalated the situation

Mastering these key areas is not hard and we can learn what's needed to make the appropriate adjustments. The question is will we make the adjustment in the moment just like Penelope did? Just because we know we should make an adjustment doesn't mean that we will actually do it. When we are overwhelmed by stress and emotion, our best intentions get pushed aside, and we may choose an easier or more convenient option. When we learn small actions to apply then we are increasing our skill level for those emotionally charged situations. This is why it's important to make a commitment to apply what we learn through continual practice. Other people's "moods" can then be an opportunity to heighten our skill set rather than a point of annoyance and emotional disruption.

Throughout the day we can stop and ask ourselves:

- "How am I feeling right now?"
- "Why am I feeling this way?"
- "How am I responding to this emotion?"

If it is positive, one should reward one's self by saying,

- "Good job. Keep up the good work."

If we feel we should handle things differently, then ask,

- "What can I do differently next time?"

Having a connection to our emotions by having awareness of how we are feeling and how those emotions are influencing our thoughts and actions is key. We need to check in often. Connect to our core emotions, especially those that we have pushed far away and do not always want to acknowledge. It is time to accept those emotions and be more comfortable with them. Having these emotions is ok. It is what you do with them that is the important factor. Having higher emotional intelligence is not turning our emotions off; it is feeling comfortable and connected to them, and responding to them in a mindful, positive way.

Never do something permanently foolish just because you are temporarily upset."

Phrase the truth in a positive, powerful way

 Write down three positive statements for every negative thought you have to strengthen your emotional intelligence. Be open with your thoughts to strengthen those that benefit you and change those that bring no value to your life and your goal for success.

Watch and Learn

We can learn so much from other people as long as we look to the right people to learn from. How do individuals with higher EQ deal with life's difficulties? We can observe them. How do individuals with higher EQ look as they are interacting with others? How are they feeling? Well, that can be a difficult one to identify just by looking, so maybe you could even ask them. Ask them, "How do you stay calm when you are presenting to a large group? How are you feeling in that situation? What goes through your mind when you are angry? What do you do to de-escalate yourself?" Their answers could change our life if we apply what we learn from them. Watch, listen, and feel it when we experience someone modeling high EQ, and start applying tiny things immediately. Body language is a good place to start. Our body language can actually change our cortisol levels in our body. Image that! My body position can change how I experience stress. Sweet!

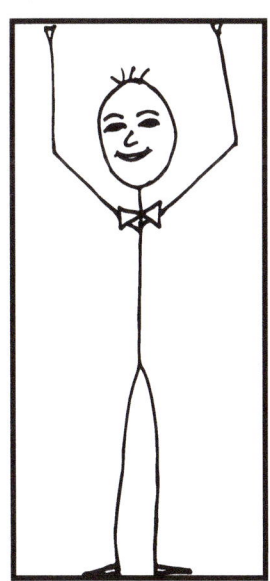 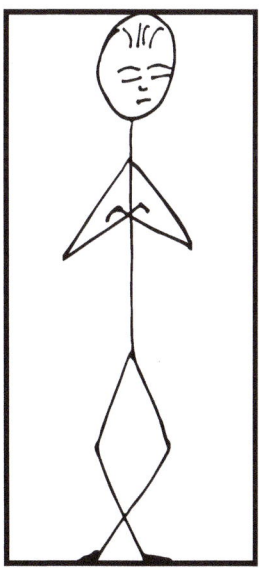

Power Posing, shown in the left picture, for two minutes can decrease our cortisol levels, which allow us to deal with stress more effectively and make better decisions. Conversely, a closed or non-confident body position, shown in the right picture, tells others and ourselves that we cannot cope with the situation at hand and it shows chemically in our increased cortisol levels. Our behavior is telling our brain how to respond…faking it until we believe it. When we feel more powerful then we are more aware of our actions and the actions of other people.

Studies show that your body language communicates up to 50 percent of what you want to say.

Folded arms, hands on hips, rapid breathing, clenched fist, staring eyes= **ANGER**
Smiling, loose, open arms, relaxed body, smiling, relaxed eye contact = **H APPY**
Leaning forward, attentive eye contact = **INTEREST**
Constant impatience, edginess, rapid breathing, fast beating heart = **ANXIOUSNESS**
Movement backward, eyebrows up, large eyes, mouth open = **SURPRISE**
Flushed face, avoiding direct eye contact, looking away, forced smile = **EMBARRASSMENT**
Focused stare, loud speech and rapid breathing = **FURY**
Slouched body, mouth turned down, dropping eyes = **SADNESS**

Write down five things that make you comfortable, and then do as many as you can.

CHANGE SEATS

Our goal is to understand others' moods, behaviors, and motives in order to increase the quality of our relationships. Keep that in mind when we are having an interaction with someone and we are irritated by that person's actions. Picture yourself in a movie theater and notice where you are sitting at the time of your interaction. Are you so close to the screen that you can only see one part of the screen at a time? Where we choose to "sit" in our interactions with others either improves the quality of our relationships or it stifles those relationships. We can choose to have a projector perspective so we can see the whole screen at one time. Changing our seat to get a better view is an option to us at any time. As soon as we feel irritated, we can get up and change our seat to get a better view. Literally changing our seat isn't required; however, it may give us a physical prompt to flip on the projector switch.

Gritty Lasagna: The Print in Blueprint

Scenario

Pete

Penelope

Pete is angry with Penelope and feels she isn't hearing him. Actually he feels like she is stifling his feelings. Pete isn't saying this exactly, but it's how he feels and it shows in his behavior. Penelope notices that Pete's behavior is escalating during their discussion even though her intent is not to upset Pete. However, Pete is not the only person in this interaction whose agitation is increasing. Penelope can feel the heat in her face as her blood pressure is rising. She could easily match Pete's behavior and blow this conversation up! As Penelope notices the heat in her face she visualizes her current seat in the movie theater. She sees that she is in the front row and can only see one section of the screen, and her reaction to that part of the screen is really aggravating her and she feels like she could have a two-year old tantrum. That thought actually amuses Penelope for a second and in her thought distraction she gets up and physically changes her seat in the room she is sharing with Pete, as well as the seat in her virtual movie theater. She is sitting way back by the projector now and has a much better view of the screen and her part in it. Penelope doesn't feel like she has to react to every word out of Pete's mouth, the tone or volume of his voice. She has created the space she needs to remind herself of her intent which is to be heard. Pete can't hear her right now because he is stuck up in the balcony next to the speaker; not to mention his angled view of the screen is obstructed. And he forgot his glasses!

Penelope was able to notice her emotional state in her interaction with Pete and choose to change it through a shift in her awareness. She used her feelings as a prompt to herself to change something. Penelope doesn't have any control over Pete's thoughts, feelings, or behavior. She may not like it, but his emotional state is not going to change just because she doesn't like it. Pete's behavior may de-escalate as a response to Penelope's choice, but that's not a guarantee. Penelope was able to de-escalate herself knowing she would be able to provide Pete with what he needed at the moment, which was for her to listen to him. Penelope was able to see that Pete wasn't in a state of mind to hear her because of the multitude of stressors affecting him. Stress affects our coping skills and our ability to see things clearly. Through Penelope's seat change she could now see that Pete's senses were diminished by his seat in the movie theater.

Give yourself individualized attention when participating in specific types of conversations such as texts, emails, and other social media time. Act, do not react. Think about your actions and the potential results before you react.

Emotional Intelligence

NO MORE WAITING

One of the easiest ways to change our mood is to do something different. If we are feeling bored, get up and take a walk listening to upbeat music. If we are disappointed, think of three things that we are grateful for in our lives. The important thing is to do something different, positive. Do not allow this negative mood or feeling carry us away. We have the ability to create our own weather, so choose a sunny, bright day over gray, gloomy one. If we start to feel angry, we can close our eyes and take a few moments to strongly imagine feeling relaxed and comfortable. What do we have to lose? Give it a try! At the very least, it will direct our attention away from our current state of mind.

Raising emotional intelligence does not need to be a difficult task. It will require a conscious effort to change the way we react emotionally to different situations, but it is so worth it! Raising emotional intelligence can bring about much opportunity and benefit to our life. Whether people are successful with managing their finances, businesses, or emotions, to get to their desired goal, the key to their success is the same. They stay in the game. They stay in the game. They STAY in the game. We will be successful in managing our emotions when we decide to stay in it. We do this by staying aware of how we are feeling and making a choice to take action based on what we want. If we don't, we can try again.

ACTIVITY

Choose How You Feel

Exercise to use when you are experiencing an emotion that you would like to change.

How would I feel if I wasn't so _____.

I would like to feel _____.

When I feel _____ things are _____ for me.

My actions are _____ when I'm feeling _____.

I like to feel _____.

So I will choose the feeling of _____ right now because _____
_____
_____.

The good news about emotional intelligence is that there isn't a limited amount to go around. There isn't a glass ceiling that needs to be broken. Emotional intelligence is about our awareness of our self and how we are being affected by our environment and circumstances. When we tap into that awareness then we know we now have choices about our reactions. The feeling may be strong. However, our choices about whether we take a step toward or away from the cupcake makes all the difference.

STRESS

Stress is the windows of a house. Stress makes our vision cloudy when not dealt with in a functional way. The windows of our house make your vision to the outside world clear or cloudy, and if we allow stress to overcome us, we can blow our windows out causing damage to ourselves, as well as, those around us by the broken glass.

STRESS

Chapter 6

More Bucket Fillers, Please!
At my children's elementary school they talk about bucket fillers and bucket dippers. Bucket fillers say positive things to their peers like "Jimmy, your science project was really cool. You did a great job!" Bucket fillers also take positive actions related to their peers like helping them pick up items that fell out of someone's desk. Bucket dippers do the opposite. They make fun of Jimmy's science project and kick the items across the room that fell out of their peer's desk. This bucket filling strategy is two-fold: it improves peer relations (we like it when people notice the things we have done well), and it increases the likelihood that we notice positives in others and ourselves. What we are doing is building coping skills that are more likely to get us more of what we want or our desired goal.

Those of us who were raised in the "survival of the fittest" era may not have been exposed to this idea on a daily basis in school. Some may have experienced bucket filling at home or in their communities. Others were bombarded with bucket dippers and then used bucket dipping as a survival technique. Fear is usually the emotion or internal factor that precedes bucket dipping. It has proven to be effective in changing behavior immediately. Parents use it, teachers use it, employers use it, advertisers use it, politicians use it, and the list goes on. What happens when our government is lead by a bunch of bucket dippers…a bunch of people who are afraid that there isn't enough? There won't be enough social security, healthcare, teachers, firemen, police officers, and therefore you will die! Okay, they don't exactly say it like that, but that is what's inferred. It's effective…we vote by emotion because we are human. Fear is an emotion that increases stress. Increased stress increases negative behaviors. When we have a whole country that is stressed then it is no wonder we see a whole lot of negative behaviors. This is the problem with bucket dipping.

> *In times of great stress or adversity, its always best to keep busy, to plow your anger and your energy into something positive.*

INCREASE STRESS = INCREASE NEGATIVE BEHAVIORS

Sometimes in moments of stress and suffering, we act in negative or harmful ways out of inner compulsions that shout too loudly in our ears to be ignored. Other times, we act on autopilot, going through the motions of a habit or behavioral pattern without much conscious thought. We are reactionary.

Having a positive outlook and ways to handle negative moments can help us create a life of greater happiness and less stress. Having increased stress leads to increased negative behaviors. By understanding the triggers and reasons for our stress, we can change our view on those things that contribute to these negative emotions. By focusing our thoughts and feelings about our stress triggers towards human happiness and emotional health, we can correct our expressive path to a resilient personal strength.

Key emotional states lead us to a more satisfactory and happy life. Gratitude, Optimism, Flow, Mindfulness, and Spirituality are traits that have a positive effect on our mindset and ultimately our actions. Pleasurable mindsets and thoughts delight the senses, make us feel better, cost nothing to do and take little effort to enjoy. But as we all know, pleasurable moments and their effects diminish overtime, so we must continue to focus our attention and efforts on a happy, positive lifestyle that we keep in the forefront of our minds and practice daily.

Write a personal affirmation on your smartphone's wallpaper so that you see it every time you pick up your phone. Post positive statements about yourself at locations such as your work bulletin board, computer monitor, or bathroom mirror.

BE CUED IN

The true source of stress isn't always obvious and it is easy to overlook stress inducing thoughts, feelings and behaviors. Constantly worrying about deadlines may stress us, but maybe it is our procrastination rather than the actual job responsibilities that lead to our deadline stress. We must look closely at our habits, attitudes and excuses, because until we take control of our stress that we can manage our stress will manage us.

Think about this. There is a certain amount of money each month to pay our bills, but the total cost of our bills at times totals more than the pot of money available. Each bill has

a due date and when the money is not available to pay the bill by the due date, this can cause stress for most people. So what if you have the choice to pay your bills whenever you want? No deadline. No minimum amount due. You can pay it or not pay in each month or pay any amount you want. This may eliminate stress for some, while others may feel a bit relieved that they can pay late without a penalty, but the financial stressor isn't totally eliminated. What may be a stressor for one person, may not be a stressor to another.

It may seem like there isn't much we can do about stress. Those monthly bills will still be due each month, there will never be more than 24 hours in a day, and family and job responsibilities will always be present. We do have more control than we think, and the realization that we are in control of our life is the foundation of stress management. Managing stress is about taking charge, and being aware of how a situation is impacting our emotions and behavior. Once we recognize the triggers of our stress, we can make an effort to modify those triggers or modify our reaction to those triggers.

We all react to stress in different ways. Some may experience psychological cues like anger, anxiety, panic, worry, cravings and loss of concentration. Others may experience physiological cues where our bodies experience responses such as tightened stomach, rapid pulse or shortness of breath. Observable changes in behavior are common and some may see an increase or decrease in eating or sleeping, increased alcohol consumption, smoking, aggressiveness, or irritability. Once we understand the changes that occur in our bodies, minds and behaviors during stressful situations, we can use these cues to signal that we are experiencing some type of stress. That signal is a heightened state of self-awareness, by the way. Once we have acknowledgment that we are experiencing stress, we can effectively control our reaction in a positive way that does not create additional stressors by incorporating stress reduction techniques that specifically work for us. Once we are able to reduce or remove the stress with these chosen techniques, we create a path to take our stress management one step further, potentially removing the stressor all together from future occurrences. Rather than just addressing the symptoms, we can take a look at our lives and explore what might be causing the stress and work at resolving it. Controlling stress is important, but if we can remove some stressors and their triggers, we will have a better quality of life.

ACTIVITY

STRESS JOURNAL

A stress journal can help you identify the regular stressors in your life and the way you deal with them. Each time you feel stressed, write them down in your journal. As you keep a daily log you will begin to see patterns and common themes. Buy a notebook or journal or download an app. Just write it down!

Answer these questions:
- What is causing your stress?
- How do you feel physically and emotionally?
- What is your behavior?
- What actions make you feel better?

FILL UP YOUR TOOLBOX

Many people cope with their stress in ways that may compound the problem so identifying effective coping skills is extremely important. Effective coping skills should be contributing to our greater emotional and physical health, and if our current coping techniques are not working, then it is time to find new ones. There are many techniques to reduce stress and choosing the ones that work best for us is vital. When dealing with a stressful situation, the goal should be to walk away from that stressor feeling better than you did before the stressor occurred, having no regrets with the way we respond. Choose what works best to make a positive change. Choice is key and change is required for stress management.

Positive coping strategies can temporarily reduce the current stress in your life, and impact the longer-term, chronic stress, as well. It may also aid in your ability to tackle day-to-day challenges, increasing your sense of confidence and your motivation too. Those who implement positive strategies in their daily lives seem to resiliently bounce back from the "rough" days and seem to be happier people, overall.

A tool to deal with stress is finding positive, effective coping strategies that work for us. Recognize that not all strategies will work for all situations. We will need a toolbox of coping strategies readily available to go to work when the need arises.

Examples of Coping Strategies:

- Make positive affirmations/statements
- Build your gratitude and focus on three things in which you are thankful
- Reduce your load and give yourself permission to say "no"
- Focus on positive communication skills
- Relax, relax, relax
- Write it all down and express yourself in writing or another creative way
- Talk to someone you trust
- Give yourself the gift of time
- Walk away and take some space
- Overcome negative self-talk
- Consider whether this issue will matter in an hour, a day, a week, a month, a year
- Learn to forgive
- Take a deep breath and release

Make a list of things that make you feel better, such as certain songs, poems, quotes, bible versus, etc. and have them ready to use when you get stressed.

ACTIVITY

Building your Tool Box: Use your best coping strategies.

- List five situations that you have recently found difficult to manage
- Write down the techniques you used to reduce stress in these situations
- Write down the results of each situation and make note of whether or not your stress was reduced mildy, moderate, greatly

Keep notes on what worked and what did not work, and you will soon figure out which strategies work for you. The goal is to find the strategies that greatly reduce your stress and those that will become a part of your Coping Skills Tool Box.

In times of great stress or adversity, its always best to keep busy, to plow your anger and your energy into something positive.

Rinse and Repeat: relax with purpose. When you get overwhelmed, relax all of your body, starting at the top of your head all the way down to your toes. Close your eyes, relax your mind, take in a very deep breath and swing your arms up over your head. Hold your breath in for 3 seconds and slowly release. As you release the breath from your body, slowly drop your hands to your sides and push the breath from the top of your head down out through your toes. Rinse and Repeat two more times for optimal results.

HOMEOSTASIS: GOOD ALL AROUND

Homeostasis is the goal of the body so it can run efficiently. Our bodies are constantly regenerating and reacting to change for homeostasis. When we think our bodies are at rest, like when we are sleeping, we are really regenerating and repairing for balance. When we put stress on our bodily system, our bodies have to work harder to run efficiently which can cause wear and tear. Mental homeostasis creates stability, calmness, and composure, which help us attain our desired outcomes or goals. When we have mental stress, our ability to stay balanced and on course becomes very difficult, if not impossible. We can constantly make small choices to help us keep our mental balance.

Scenario

Penelope wants to start her new exercise plan of working out for one hour, five times per week. It's been about fifteen years since she followed this type of exercise plan despite her many efforts. Penelope believes this time is different and has put an exercise plan together for the week. She will start tomorrow, Monday, after work and will attend a yoga class at 5:30pm. Penelope is feeling confident this plan will be successful as she packs her workout bag for the next day.

Monday at 4pm, Penelope is wrapping up her workday and is anxiously waiting on 5pm and then will be on her way to the gym. Her boss pops his head in her office and asks her to complete a short brief before she leaves today. Penelope happily accepts the work, which takes her mind off the time, and she is able to make progress quickly because she has written thousands of briefs in her career. Penelope's work is interrupted by a phone call from her daughter, Penny, who is stranded at her school because her ride went home sick today. Penelope knows she cannot leave work now, meet her boss's deadline, and get to her yoga class by 5:30pm. She mutters to herself, "I'm not missing my yoga class!" It takes her six phone calls before she can actually talk to a real person who can pick up Penny. It's 5:05pm and Penelope finally finishes the brief and knows she can quickly make the five copies her boss needs, place it on his desk, get changed, and make it to her yoga class which is fifteen minutes away.

Penelope

Penelope places the brief on the copier and hits the button, and she is on her way to her office to get her gym bag and quickly get changed into her yoga clothes. As Penelope gets to the hall she hears the copier stop and she runs back to check that she hit five copies. She did, but the copier is jammed and tears her original while trying to get it out of the machine. Penelope decides to reprint five copies in her office and deal with the paper jam tomorrow. After she places the sealed envelope with the five copies of the brief in her boss's office, Penelope runs to her office to get her purse and is off to the parking garage via the elevator.

Once she gets to the parking garage, Penelope realizes she has forgotten to change and her workout bag is still in her office. She heads back to her office and it is 5:30pm by the time Penelope gets in her car. Penelope quickly does the math and knows she can be in yoga class in twenty minutes; she takes a deep breath and decides forty minutes is still a good workout for day one. As Penelope pulls onto the highway she finds herself in bumper-to-bumper traffic. She feels defeated and can't wait to get home and take a nap.

Stress

When Penelope said she wanted to start exercising five times a week for one hour a day, even though she hadn't exercised like this in fifteen years, failure was right around the corner for her as the home and work stressors hit her at all at once. We can feel Penelope's pain because we have been in this snowball effect before. We may push through to meet our exercise goal, but eventually something breaks the exercising cycle for many of us. Sometimes it's circumstances that mess up our timed expectations like Penelope's, or sometimes it's our body that actually breaks down and gets sick and now we couldn't go to the gym if we wanted to, which we don't! Many times our "new exercise plan" goes to pot because our equilibrium is thrown off as the running list in our mind grows by the minute. Apply immense pressure over and over again without additional supports and things break down, crumble to the ground, and our plans go with it. Our current behavior is the best indicator of our skill set. If our behavior is telling us that we don't exercise five times a week for an hour then change the expectation until it is in alignment with our behavior.

Penelope could have changed her exercise plan once she realized she had to go back to her office to get her workout clothes. Ultimately, Penelope doesn't care what type of exercise she does, so how could she have turned her situation around to take a baby step towards her long-term exercise goal? Yoga class is one way to move, but it wasn't Penelope's only movement option. We aren't the best at brainstorming ideas when we are all stressed out; we actually get more tunnel vision. When we can create mental homeostasis by brainstorming ideas before our exercise plan gets crushed or taking some calming yoga breaths in the moment, our pathway becomes clear so we can then go around the speed bumps and keep putting one foot in front of another, metaphorically and literally.

Keep your effecting coping skills with you so they can be accessed when needed. Example: if a song calms you down, make sure it is on your phone, so that you can listen to it at any time, when you may need it.

We are a soul. We have a body.

Practice Pleasure

We are not always given the exact circumstances that we wish for at all times, but by finding pleasure in the situations presented, we can relieve ourselves of unnecessary stress. Finding pleasure and gratitude in the smallest things in our life help us stay happy and positive.

Scenario

Penelope

Stressed Mom

Penelope was sitting at the pool while on vacation and observed a woman who seemed very stressed interacting with her children. This lady was angry, frustrated and yelling at the kids, because she wanted them to leave her alone and allow her to relax. A little while later, Penelope noticed this stressed mother watching a smiling mom who was enjoying her children and finding pleasure in the moment she was given. After a little while, the smiling mom got out of the pool, walked over to her lounge chair and relaxed. The children allowed her to have her own time and played in the pool with one another. Penelope looked back towards the stressed mom, and noticed that she took a deep breath, started to smile and played with her children joyfully. After about 15 minutes, she walked over to her lounge chair and laid down to relax, while he children played together in the pool.

By the smiling mom giving her children some attention and enjoying her time with the children, she was able to better enjoy her vacation, and in the end gets the opportunity to relax on her own. She did all of this without any negativity and added stress.

These small blessings are everywhere we turn and today's technology plays a huge role in simplifying many daily tasks. Pleasure can be found in the simple task of doing our laundry. Yes, we can be grateful for laundry! Grateful that we can open a lid on a washing machine, fill the premeasured cup up with laundry detergent which has already been formulated to not only clean our clothes but make them smell mountain fresh, retain their vibrant colors, and soften our fabric so our skin doesn't get chafed. Conversely, we could be collecting all of our dirty clothes in a durable bag or basket and carrying them by foot to the nearest body of fresh water. Washing clothes on rocks or a fancy washboard takes a lot of time and energy. So the next time we are in our homes and getting ready to "do the laundry" with a sigh, we can use the push, pull, or turn of a knob as a reminder that if we can find pleasure and gratitude in doing the laundry then imagine all the possibilities for the rest of the day. Just think of all the small things we do before we leave our home in the morning. Being optimistic and staying in that positive flow over time becomes a habit, an automatic way of life.

It really doesn't matter if you see the glass half empty or half full. It's more important to be grateful that you have something to drink.

Personal Affirmations

This has been stated numerous times, no self-defeating talk allowed. We need to focus on the positive and grow from a strength-base place. Create a list of affirmations that represent individual strengths. "I am a determined individual who can reach a goal." Stating my characteristic in positive terms will reinforce how I can bring about positive change. I need to focus on positive aspects of who I am and be appreciative of what I do well. If I feel like I have some traits that are viewed questionable, then write them down by identifying the times when this trait would be considered a positive. " My assertive nature keeps me on track to reach my desired goals no matter what."

If you want to achieve a goal then start with your strengths and not your weaknesses. That seems reasonable, but many times we start with the very thing we are not good at doing. "I'm not very good at managing my money, so I'll try to be better starting this week". Start with your weakness of managing money and speaking in "we'll see" language is a sure fire way to fail! We want to affirm our desire and act and speak "as if". "As if" it is already true! Maybe "I'm great at managing my money" is too far of a stretch, so adjust your affirmation to the degree right before your immediate response is "that's a lie". For example, I'm working at managing my finances every day with small choices I make, and it feels good to be on the road to financial stability!"

Stressors are everywhere! Our goal isn't to eliminate all stressors because we would stress ourselves out trying. We don't have control over other people, our genetics, or natural disasters. The effects of these internal or external factors can definitely increase our stress level, but being aware of our emotions gives us cues to start putting those coping strategies to work so our vision isn't clouded. Balance is achieved through practice; noticing the ease of your breath or the beauty of a flower are simple steps of gratitude. The laws of physics are always at work; by the action of filling just one person's bucket to the top, it can't help but to spill over into our own bucket.

Communication

Communication is the doors of a house. Communication is the access between the inside and outside world. Like the door to our house, it is the gateway to others.

Gritty Lasagna: The Print in Blueprint

COMMUNICATION

CHAPTER 7

 *I remember telling my kids years ago, that talking to them was like the Abbott and Costello comedy skit, 'Who's on First'. I could not make heads or tails of what they were communicating that day. They had never heard of this skit, so I played it for them; years later, it is on their iPods and they still listen to it for a good chuckle. If you have never heard this routine before, Google it. Many videos, sounds bites and written scripts are available on the Internet of this 1930's comedy bit. It portrays a classic version of miscommunication. The premise behind the exchange shows Costello as a ballpark vendor talking with Abbott, who is the manager of a baseball team. Abbott wants to make sure Costello knows the name of the players before he goes down onto the field to interact with the team. As Abbott begins to recite the names of the players, Costello gets confused for reasons quickly realized and the laughing from the audience begins. I recommend that you actually watch the video. Don't just listen or read the script. Neither does it justice. The words alone are funny, but seeing the character's actions and reactions during the dialogue, tell a much bigger story. Seeing the interaction between the two comedians complete the interaction and illustrate a perfect example of communication gone wrong. The skit is a very funny way of showing how a simple interaction can go south very quickly. It reiterates how important good communication skills are to any interaction and that good communication goes far beyond the actual words spoken. Abbott and Costello are funny, but confusion in real day-to-day interactions is no laughing matter. Poor communication results in anger, hurt feelings, and possibly broken relationships. There is an inside joke in my house. When someone is communicating poorly and it is confusing to understand, we say, "Who's on first?" For those that understand the joke, it is a cue to evaluate our communication skills at that moment, and for those that don't know the joke, it helps us personally from getting upset, and allows us to react to this poor interaction from a more positive state of mind.*

NO COMEDY SKIT HERE

Good communication skills are key to success in life, work and relationships. Without effective communication, a message can turn into an error, misunderstanding, frustration, or even disaster by being misinterpreted or poorly delivered. How many of us have ever had a friend say something and our immediate reaction was anger? But after we thought about what our friend said again, we realized our initial reaction was incorrect. Once we had a moment to think about their comment, we could see their true intent more clearly the second time? Sometimes assumptions are made by the speaker and we do not understand the true meaning. Consequently, we react negatively, allowing the situation to quickly become an issue. This is an example of how a piece of information can be misinterpreted from a poor delivery.

 The difference between the right word and the almost right word is the difference between lightning and a lightning bug." - Mark Twain

Communication is the exchange of information between individuals or groups of people and involves listening, as well as speaking. When we speak to others, how we deliver our message plays a major part in how it is received by others. It is a process where we try as clearly and accurately as we can to convey our thoughts, intentions and objectives. Communication is successful only when both the sender and the receiver understand the same information with the same intent. If the same understanding is not there, problems occur, having a huge impact on the relationship, whether it is business or personal.

Excellent communication skills are a benefit in every area of life, but many of us have not yet mastered these skills. It is not hard to look around and realize those who still have a struggle in this area. The inability to communicate effectively will hold these individuals back in their work, social and personal relationships. Business and personal relationships rely heavily on social exchanges and those with above-average communication skills often come out ahead. Without effective communication techniques, we can have communication pitfalls that undermine our good work and interfere with fostering positive relationships. But don't fret because communication skills are something that we can develop and fine tune.

"You can change your world by changing your words... Remember, death and life are in the power of the tongue." — Joel Olstean

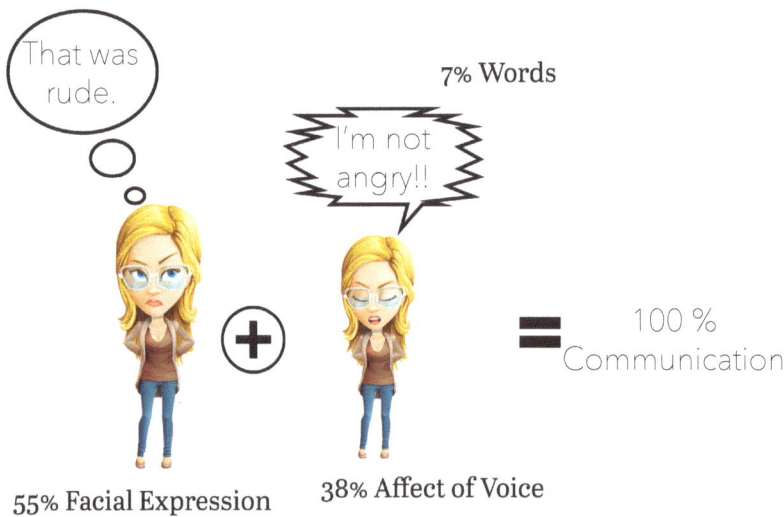

THE COMMUNICATION EQUATION

55% Facial Expression + 38% Affect of Voice = 100 % Communication

(7% Words)

Hit the pause button before you respond.

A Look Says It All

Communication is both verbal and nonverbal. Verbal communication consists of the sounds and language that relay a message. This is considered the actual words we use and sounds that represent words. Non-verbal is EVERYTHING else.

Nonverbal communication is the process of communication through sending and receiving wordless cues, which are mainly visual, between individuals. Nonverbal communication, such as our facial expressions, gestures, body spacing, eye contact, posture, pitch, inflection, rhythm, rate of speech, and tone of voice, speak the loudest. It is referred to as body language, but nonverbal communication encompasses much more, such as, speed in which we speak, use of voice volume, touch, distance, physical environments, and appearance. The way we listen, look, move, and react tells the other person whether or not we care, if we are being truthful, and how well we are listening to them. When our nonverbal signals match up with the words we are saying, they increase trust, clarity, and rapport. When they don't, they generate tension, mistrust, and confusion. Nonverbal communication involves the processes of encoding and decoding. Encoding is the act of generating the information such as facial expressions, gestures, and postures. Decoding is the interpretation of information from received sensations from previous experiences. Typically overlooked in nonverbal communication is proximity or the informal space around the body. Eye contact is comprised of the action of looking while talking and listening, frequency of glances, patterns of fixation, pupil dilation, and blink rate. The actual words of a message play a smaller role in the intention and meaning of that message than we may realize. We have to consider an individual's facial expression, tone in their voice, and body language to get a clearer picture of the message's true meaning and the messenger's intent. Communication between individual's is greatly improved when the whole communication equation is considered.

We all have had interactions when the words a person was saying did not jive with their voice tone, the look on their face, or the stance of their body. When this happens, it is a clear example of poor message delivery and an open door for a communication misunderstanding to occur. What one does says more than the words one chooses to use. Nonverbal communication accounts largely for what is seen and understood by a listener, not what is heard. Nonverbal communication is the cues that guide the true meaning. It helps clarify and add depth to the spoken words. It is the occurrence of talking without speaking and plays a powerful role in one's ability to communicate effectively. When verbal communication and nonverbal communication agree, the message that is being communicated is better understood allowing us to reach our goal of CLEAR Communication.

> "What you do speaks so loud that I can not hear what you say." -Ralph Waldo Emerson

The steps for *CLEAR* Communication

C = Consider and clearly know what to say and why.
Understand the purpose and intent of the message. Know with whom we are communicating and why. Consider any barriers we may encounter such as cultural differences or situational circumstances (gender, age, or economic biases). Ask ourselves what outcome we want to achieve and the impression we want to leave.

L = Language choice, to know how we will say our message.
Begin by making eye contact. We inspire trust and confidence when we look a person in the eyes when speaking. Second, be aware of our body language since it can say as much, or more, than our words. By standing with arms easily at the side we tell others that we are approachable and open to hearing what they have to say. If instead, our arms are crossed and shoulders hunched, it suggests disinterest or unwillingness to communicate. Good posture and an approachable stance help make even difficult communication flow more smoothly. Make sure to speak in a cooperative, non-adversarial tone. Be nonjudgmental.

E = Emotions should be checked.
Recognize our own emotional state. Can we say what we need to say without allowing our feelings positively or negatively impacting our purpose. When we are angry and do not feel like we are in full control of our emotions, we have to recognize that this may not be the best time to communicate our message to others. On the other hand, there are times when showing emotion is acceptable and may be needed for examples, if we are trying to share our condolences with someone whose husband has died, showing empathy is appropriate; otherwise, we would appear uncaring.

A =Actively listen to others.
Communication is a two way street. After we have said what we have to say, stop, listen, and look for feedback and clues for comprehension. While the person is responding, avoid any impulses to cut the speaker off and avoid listening only for the end of their sentence, so that we can blurt out more ideas or thoughts that have come to our mind. Respectfully give the speaker our full attention. When they are finished, we can ensure that our message has been clearly and correctly understood by asking open-ended questions that encourage continued discussion.

R =Reach an understanding, agreement or consensus with those involved.
Once we have had the opportunity to discuss our message and consider the feedback received, re-visit the purpose of the interchange. Have we reached common ground, solved a problem, or clarified our position? If the purpose was to teach or instruct, have we accomplished our goal? To communicate well is to understand and be understood. Make sure that our message has been received as intended and that any questions or concerns have been alleviated. We can even agree to disagree. There are no guarantees that our communication efforts will be met with total compliance and agreement. As long as we understand each other, are cordial and respectful, we can still have a successful exchange.

ACTIVE LISTENING

Active listening begins with the ears, not the mouth. Rather than responding instinctively to what another person is saying, take the time to listen to them and understand the situation. It is important to make sure the other person feels heard and understood. Be present and engaging, don't just hear. To make a person feel heard, make eye contact, ask relevant questions, minimize distractions, and generally give the impression that what the person is saying is important. Knowing how to listen properly is one of the most important skills we can have.

We should be listening to understand, learn and obtain information, but research shows that a person typically remembers only up to 50% of what is said to them from a conversation 10 minutes prior. Really, in 10 minutes we can only recall 50% of what was said to us? Why? Because many individuals are not good listeners and do not participate in ongoing active listening. Good communication skills require a higher level of self-awareness and a conscious effort to hear not only the words that another is saying, but to understand the complete meaning of the message that is being given. Asking questions like Who, What, When, Where, and Why, not only allow us to obtain the information for gaining a full understanding of the message, but it also shows the messenger that we are actively involved in the communication process. We are showing them that what they are saying matters. When speaking to others, we want to know that they are truly listening and paying attention to what we have to say, so giving this same respect to others when they are speaking is important.

"There is no greater gift to give to someone than your interest." – Anonymous

ACTIVITY

Being Present Takes Practice

A practical thing that you can do to practice active listening is be present and embrace the moment.

Enroll a friend or someone you work with to practice with you.

Have them tell you a story, and use your active listening skills to engage in the conversation. Have them give you feedback on their observations to learn what you do well, and what you can learn to do better.

Scenario

Penelope's teenage daughter's friend, Sara, comes over to their house. Sara is in rare form; she is usually very calm and level-headed, but she is in a rage today. Sara starts ranting about her mother, Susie, and how she has been nit-picking at her all week and Sara can't take it anymore. Sara is a very good high school student, is involved in several clubs, plays soccer, and has a part time job, were she has been promoted twice in the last year. She is a responsible, organized, and overall great teenager. Penelope is very happy her daughter, Penny, is friends with Sara. However, Susie can be an overbearing and perfectionist parent and has a tendency to be overly critical of her well-rounded daughter. In other words, Penelope understands Sara's frustrations with her mother and wants to support her angst; however, Penelope wouldn't want another parent fueling her own daughter's fury with her. Therefore, Penelope calmly says that she can see that Sara is very upset and asks her if she wants to sit down in their living room and tell Penelope and Penny what happened. Sara gives them an overview of the week and then gives a blow-by-blow of the morning accounts. Sara is talking quickly and is highly agitated while telling Penelope and Penny about how her mother snapped at her this morning about sleeping in until 7:30am, complaining that she used too much water while showering, yelled at her to get the wet towel (that just left her head 30 seconds ago) off the floor, fussed at her about her outfit choice, advised her to not eat any carbs for breakfast because Sara was getting too puffy in the face, and then called Sara lazy when she was taking a few minutes to text a friend back. It was only 9:05am on Saturday morning!

Penelope

Sara

Penelope and Penny are giving Sara their full attention by maintaining eye contact, leaning forward, nodding that they understand, asking clarifying questions, and they don't give advice about how Sara should handle her mother, nor do they defend or give their opinion about the actions of Susie. They asked questions like "you said it has been like this for the last week, so what does a typical Saturday look like in your house?" and "I know you typically have a busy schedule, but is there anything else going on with you this week?" They continue on with periodic questions as they watch Sara's body relax and her voice tone and volume return to normal. Sara shares that she has picked up some extra hours at work this week because her mom's work hours were cut three weeks ago. Sara wants to be helpful to her family and be able to pay for her cell phone, car insurance, clothes, and extracurricular activities. She has had less sleep this week because she still has schoolwork, soccer practice, and her clubs to manage. Sara realizes that she hasn't shared any of this information with her mother because she didn't want her mom to feel worse than she currently does. Now that Sara is calm she has devised a plan about how she will approach her mother and will have a discussion about what's been going on in her life and how she was feeling this morning. Sara has now been at their house for 90 minutes and Penelope and Penny have spoken very little within that timeframe. Nonetheless, Sara is grateful for their assistance and leaves relaxed and smiling.

Penelope and Penny did a great job of actively listening to Sara. Penny quickly realized that her level-headed friend needed a chance to calm down and didn't need her to throw gasoline on the fire. Keeping our mouths shut and our ears open allows the other person time to reflect and come up with their own conclusions and many times solutions that fit their own goal. Active listening isn't waiting for someone to stop talking so we can start talking. That's active talking and most people don't want to be talked at…we want to be communicated with. So how can we become a better active listener?

Here's what good, active listeners do:

- Face the speaker. Sit up straight or lean forward slightly to show our attentiveness through body language.
- Maintain eye contact and remain comfortable. This is not staring someone down.
- Minimize external distractions. Turn off the TV. Put down the book or magazine, and ask the speaker and other listeners to do the same.
- Respond appropriately to show genuine understanding by expressing a murmur ("uh-huh" and "um-hmm") and nod. Raise our eyebrows. Say words such as "Really?," "Interesting," as well as, ask information-gathering questions like, "What did you do then?" and "What did she say?"
- Focus solely on what the speaker is saying. Try not to think about our response. The conversation will follow a logical flow after the speaker makes their point.
- Minimize internal distractions. If our own thoughts start creeping in, simply let them go and continuously re-focus our attention on the speaker.
- Keep an open mind. Wait until the speaker is finished before making a decision or considering an opinion. Try not to make assumptions about what the speaker is thinking. Trust the words they are saying.
- Avoid giving an opinion to the speaker on how they should handle the situation. Unless they specifically ask for advice, assume they just need to talk it out.
- If the speaker is launching a complaint against us, wait until they finish before defending our position. The speaker will feel as though their point had been heard. They won't feel the need to repeat it, and we'll know the whole argument before we respond.
- Engage and ask questions for clarification, but, once again, wait until the speaker has finished talking, so that we don't interrupt their train of thought. After asking questions, paraphrase their point to make sure we understand their message. Start with saying, "So you're saying…".
- Allow silence and use it to better understand all points of view. Don't feel the need to always say something. Allow natural pauses in the conversation to occur. Don't worry about what we should do or say next while they are speaking.

Ask 2 questions of others when they are done talking before you say anything you would like to say in response.

How to Get our Voice Heard

Human beings are social beings and individuals interact with others every day. Often, our happiness depends a great deal on how the interactions with each person play out. This is especially true of those whom we care about. However, because each person has a unique personality, disagreements are normal, even in the best of relationships.

To have good management of relationships, we need to be assertive and honest in sharing our thoughts, feelings and concerns. However, this needs to be done in a way that does not provoke the other person and should stay respectful, encouraging both parties to listen to each other. How we present our grievances can make the difference between resolving a dispute or can add to the hostility. If we want the other person to listen to our complaint and be fair in their response, we can communicate our concern in a non-provocative approach. A good way to do this is through the communication technique of "I" Messages VS. "You" Messages.

"I" messages statements are made about ourselves, how we feel, address our concerns, and state what actions from the other person led to our concerns. "You" messages focus on the other person and would usually lead them to becoming defensive unless the "You" message is a positive statement about the other person.

Scenario

Penelope

Penelope is waiting for Pete to come home from work so they can immediately leave for Paul's school music concert. When Pete arrives, Penelope states, "You are always coming home late! Why can't you come home on time?" Pete gets angry and storms out of the room.

Pete

The "You" message, Penelope statement leaves Pete feeling blamed and attacked, subsequently resulting in a non-friendly response from Pete. In a conflict, "You" messages put others on the defense resulting in the original concerns being pushed aside. Because Pete feels attacked by Penelope's "You" message, the issue now for Pete is the way Penelope addressed her concerns and not the issue of Pete coming home late. Pete does not hear Penelope's concerns because of her approach, and his energy is focused on defending himself.

If Penelope had used an "I" message instead, she would have said to Pete, "I feel frustrated when we arrive at school functions late. I'm concerned that our son will feel unimportant when you come home late on days that are very special to him. I feel helpless wondering when you're going to be home." With an "I" message, Penelope shared her feelings and concerns without attacking Pete, providing an opportunity to discuss the issue. Clear communication of any concern is a good starting point to work things out.

ACTIVITY

Writing an Effective "I" Message

Parts to an "I" message:

I feel _____ (express your feeling)
when you _____ (describe the action that affects you or relates to the feeling)
because _____ (explain how the action affects you or relates to the feeling)

And

Sometimes a fourth part might be added. This states our preference for what we would like to take place instead.
  ...and I would like _____.

It would be nice if we never had relationship problems with others, but we will, so learning to manage them is best. Using "I" messages to communicate concerns is great way to handle everyday interpersonal difficulties that arise. Communicating our annoyance, irritation, frustration, and anger in a more controlled fashion is an effective outlet for our negative feelings, and this will likely result in less negative reactions from others that may serve only to perpetuate the relationship problems. By focusing on how the actions of others affect us personally, we are sharing the impact without placing blame, and creating a path for open communication to occur.

FEEDBACK OTHERS WILL HEAR

Feedback is received in a number of ways, both formally and informally. Formal feedback is received from supervisors, clients, colleagues, and from others in our professional relationships. Informal feedback is received from family, friends, and others in our daily environment, excluding our professional life. Feedback is essential for our personal growth. It provides opportunities to vary or amend our approach, produce better results, enhance our performance, enrich relationships, aid communication and provide guidance. If so much good comes from receiving feedback, why does feedback have such a negative connotation and feared by so many people? It is because there is a fundamental difference between constructive feedback and destructive criticism.

Constructive feedback provides information about behavior and expectations against objective standards in a way that the recipient maintains a positive attitude towards oneself and provides encouragement. Destructive criticism dominates only when things go wrong and is often personal and subjective.

Feedback Skills:

1. Differentiating between facts and emotions

It is important to differentiate between our own feelings on the matter and the facts. If our own feelings have been aroused it is possible that we will allow these to shade the facts. As a result we start becoming opinionated, using words like "must" and "should have." This has an effect on our listener, who may then exhibit a defensive behavior.

2. Positive and negative feedback

Feedback is often perceived positively or negatively but it can be constructive. For this we can provide evidence to support our statements and then together decide how one can either build on good behavior or improve bad behavior.

3. Giving feedback

When structuring your feedback try the following:
- Start with the positive. Make factual statements that show we value the person
- Comment on the specific behavior of concern
- Aim to address the important areas first, prioritizing the most pressing behaviors. There may be additional concerns, but people are demoralized if given a lot of negative feedback at once time
- Allow people to explore the implications of their behavior
- Own the feedback we give, but be aware it is only one perception, so listen for any alternative view and do not prejudge
- Think of a recent occasion on which we gave feedback, and reflect on effectiveness

4. Receiving feedback

When on the receiving end of feedback adopt the following behaviors:
- Listen to what is being said without arguing or interrupting no matter how much we disagree
- Check understanding by clarifying information rather than making assumptions
- Consult an individual for unbiased opinion to validate or invalidate the feedback
- Consider the last occasion on which we received feedback, and think about our application of the information given and how can we improve

Using the Oreo Effect when giving feedback helps to begin and to end the conversation on a positive note. When using the Oreo Effect, first start by stating something positive and factual about the person, then express the negative or constructive feedback, followed by ending with another positive, factual statement. Give them the whole Oreo, not just the pieces!

The cookie parts are the positives and the cream is the constructive feedback. We appreciate our good friends because they will "tell us how it is" while acknowledging our good parts too. All the pieces of an Oreo are the good parts, but if someone slapped crème on us then most would immediately try to get it off. We may not appreciate the gesture… we're probably annoyed by it! Unlike unasked for criticisms that don't point to any redeeming quality we may have, the Oreo Effect allows us to hear the feedback because we all want to hear a positive about ourselves and that brings our attention to the feedback. When the last thing we hear is positive about ourselves then unconsciously we are more likely to put attention on the thing we are not doing very effectively because we know when we improve that it will be recognized and appreciated. Yes, we would like the whole Oreo, please.

Giving and receiving feedback are important skills in being successful. If done well it can help to develop an open and trusting relationship benefiting both parties. If done poorly, or not done at all, it encourages attacking and defensive behavior, which will surely result in a breakdown in the communication process, as well as the relationship.

OREO EFFECT

POSITIVE
then
NEGATIVE
then
POSITIVE

When giving feedback, sandwich the negative feedback in between positive feedback. Start with something positive and end with something positive.

ROADBLOCKS TO COMMUNICATION SUCCESS

Various barriers exist that can distort or prohibit a message from being properly understood or sent. These barriers can cause conflict in interpersonal relationships, prevent a business from being successful, and lead to low employee satisfaction in an organization. Identifying the barriers to communication is the first step to improving the effectiveness of the communication. Barriers to communication are defined as, "aspects of or conditions that interfere with effective exchange of ideas or thoughts." When these barriers exist,

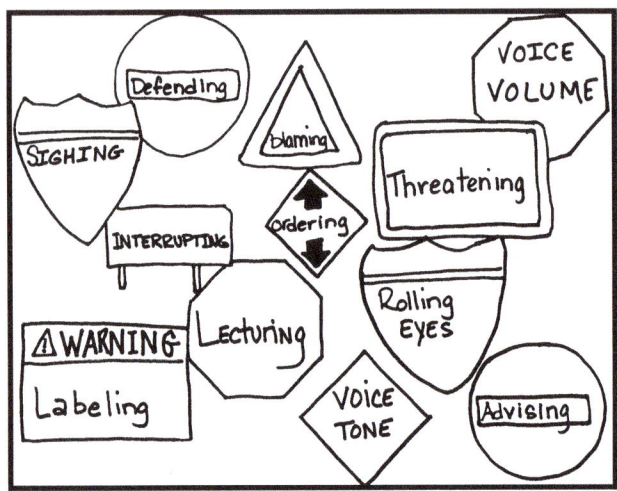

they become a roadblock. They have a tendency to shut down communication rather than open up pathways and should be avoided in conversations when possible.

Plenty of barriers can stand in our way and keep us from reaching our communication goals. Combine a few of these roadblocks into one conversation and we can easily build the Great Wall of China in no time. Visualize getting our message on the other side of a 26-foot high wall, and it is easy to see how difficult these roadblocks interfere with our goal. A variety of times our need to be right and our need to make sure others know we are right prompt us to use many of the roadblock concerns. It is irrelevant if we are right or not. Being right and pushing our opinion on others typically pushes others away and creates a shutdown of active

listening. This is the exact opposite result of what we want when we are communicating with others. Our best bet is to eliminate these items from our communication, altogether.

Power Of Healthy Words

Earlier we discussed the communication equation and stated that our words play a smaller part in the act of communication. One may walk away from this thinking the words an individual speaks does not matter, and this would be incorrect. Words are important elements of oral communication. The words used determine what we receive, how we think, and the accuracy with which we communicate thoughts and feelings. In oral communication, meanings are relayed or affected by the way we say the words, by the tone of our voice, and by our body movements. Yet, the words themselves must mean the same thing to the listener that they do to the speaker if we want to achieve effective and accurate communication. If we want positive results, then healthy words is the way to go.

Words have tremendous power to build, or they have the power to destroy. When we use words we have the power to change how we and others feel simply by the words we choose to describe our experience or feelings. By using words in a positive and healthy way, our communication with others will dramatically increase its value. How many times a day are we asked, "How's it going?" And how many times do we say, "Fine?". Typically this happens in passing and neither person even thinks about what is being said, and beyond that, there is no emotional connection. One simple way to make that exchange electric and fun is to use positive words. Using positive words in this case changes the entire experience. So when someone asks us, "How's it going?" what can our response be? We can plan ahead what we will say, and that we want it to be dramatic and impactful. Our response has the power to help another feel wonderful, and at the same time break the mental pattern of the person who asked the question. What we really want is to have the person almost become puzzled at our answer because they've never heard that type of response before. It is a lot of fun when this happens. Begin each day with the exact response that will be used, and use it every time someone asks us that question.

For example, " I feel absolutely fantastic today!" Notice how people react. If we can get a smile out of them, we are on the right track. Before long, we will feel differently in a very positive and powerful way. Words are more powerful than most people imagine. Using healthy, positive words in a powerful way gives us an enormous advantage to control the outcome of every interaction and a great start to a pleasurable life.

Simply learning how to communicate will not accomplish anything, and all the classes in the world will not make the skills come naturally. However, if the communication skills are practiced, these techniques will become habitual. Improving communication skills often consists of a series of small, concrete steps. Take things one step at a time and practice each step until it comes naturally. Knowledge, plus practice, makes all the difference.

ACTIVITY

Impactful Word List

1. Create a list of 100 healthy, positive words and choose a new one to use every day.
2. Select 5-10 words from the list and post them somewhere that can see them every day. Tack them up on a work bulletin board, hang them onto the front of the refrigerator, put them on sticky notes, and hang them around your computer monitor.
3. Select a list of characteristics you believe a happy person exhibits or consider the descriptive words that represent a positive experience in your life. These words invoke meaning and emotion, and provide the drive that is needed to stay focused on your goals.

Gritty Lasagna: The Print in Blueprint

What we say is important, but how we say it and our non-verbals really tell the whole story. Actively listening instead of actively talking provides a better understanding of what others are trying to communicate, and it gives us time to formulate our feedback in a way that will actually be heard. Isn't that the pupose of verbally communication, after all?. Once we have the tools to be an effective communicator, we can engage with others in a way that renders *Who's On First* a bonding piece of comedy instead a way of life.

CHOICE

Choice is the appliances, furnishings, etc. This concept represents the tools we need to make our house comfortable. The furnishings, appliances, etc., that are needed to help us get through life more easily. When our appliances are not functioning properly or if the leg of our couch is broken, some type of change must take place to bring things back to our Cinque. Without the ability to use our tools, we soon are living in a chaotic state.

CHOICE

 *Growing up, life wasn't always ideal. Day in and day out as a child, I would look around at my schoolmates and fantasize what their lives were like. It was a way of escaping reality for a moment by creating an alternate vision. Life threw me quite a few curve balls when I was a kid, and I always felt like I needed to prepare to dodge the next pitch. I was young and wasn't exactly sure what I considered an ideal life. I knew I did not want to have my life continue in certain ways indefinately. I knew something had to change. Being so young, I did not know what I wanted my life to be, but I was very clear about what I did not want it to be. I was very aware of the things that made me feel bad, ugly, and negative. I hated feeling "bad," so I made choices for the things that made me feel "good." Even when those pitches came out of nowhere, I worked hard to not get caught in the "woe is me" thinking that only made me feel worse. I would find the silver lining in that rogue pitch, because that type of positive thinking gave me some hope, some way of understanding and it made me feel better. Feeling better was always my goal. Because I could not control a lot of factors in my life as a child, I made much effort to control the things I could, which was always, me, myself and I. My focus was finding a place where the curve balls weren't so harmful. To do this, I had to make choices in my thinking and in my behavior that limited my time in the negative world. As I got older, I continued to make choices that would make me happy and bring joy to my life. Sometimes my choices did not exactly work out like I had planned, but as long as I could see the value in that experience, the silver lining, I was ok. It's hard living in a positive state of mind at all times, but that is always my goal. When I go to the dark side, I work really hard to bring myself back into the light. It just feels better to be in the light. I choose to live in the light. I choose to live by my life feeling, and I choose to maintain my power to control my destiny, understanding that it isn't about getting there; it's all about the journey. I choose to have my journey filled with positive moments that I create in my thinking and in my behavior. So far, this has worked well for me. I have more joys in my adult life than I could have ever imagined as a child. If it wasn't for the need to live in a happy place in my mind, I believe that things would look very different today. I give credit to a very special woman in my life, my Grandma Lombardi, who has been in heaven for some time now. Many years ago, though, she showed me that having a life with little means, did not dictate the amount of happiness in my life. It was all my choice, whether I allowed it to define me or guide me.*

 When something bad happens you have 3 choices. You can either let it define you, let it destroy you, or let it strengthen you."

Choosing Change

We have all had our fair share of storms to weather. We have dealt with a lot of stuff, sometimes the same stuff, more times than we care to admit, with escalating consequences until we finally learn the lesson. Did we learn anything along the way? We often need to change before we have to change, because when things are going along fine and dandy, there is no incentive to make those changes. When things are going well, we have no reason to make any adjustments. Then one day it happens. Some people are faced with a breaking point situation such as fighting with a loved one, gaining 20 pounds, cheating on a spouse or losing a promotion because of the inability to control personal behavior. It is at this point that individuals usually recognize that something must change. In addition, the negative consequences resulting from the trigger event, must be dealt with, too.

We can easily see the need to change a behavior in others, but often have great difficulty recognizing those similar traits in ourselves. It is easier to point fingers at others than to acknowledge the same traits in us. This is unfortunate, but true. In moments like this, we have forgotten that we are 100% responsible for our current reality. Knowing this, why would we not choose a positive, happy existence, and want to make the needed changes in ourselves sooner than later? Maybe it is because we are not self-aware, or because we have some awareness, but do not always make the best decisions. Now is the time to choose better. Time to make better decisions. Time to choose to be better today than we were yesterday. It is only through our conscious efforts to learn, grow and improve that positive change can occur. Those who loathe or ignore change ultimately become the "victims". Those who embrace change gain control, manage a positive life, and create healthy habits. They become the true architect of their own lives.

 I try to look at my growth this way: if I am not changing, then I am not growing. If I am not growing, I am falling behind in my quest to be the best "me" I can. When we are merrily going through life and everything appears great, then our need to change anything about ourselves is the last thing on our minds. Successful personal growth requires an ongoing commitment to change, adjustments in the very things that are potentially holding us back. Let's face it, we all make mistakes, play our part in a list of negative interactions or unconsciously exhibit a slew of bad habits. We forget that our actions, attitudes and behavior show the world the person we really are. Want to show the world something different? Then a change to create the life we want is a must. It is about finding value in personal development and working daily towards personal growth.

Emotion always has its roots in the unconscious and manifests itself in the body."
- Irene Claremont de Castillejo

Have gratitude for what you have in life right now. Minimally, be grateful to be alive. Challenge yourself to take a few moments every day to really appreciate what makes you happy and give thanks for it. It could be as simple as waking up in a warm bed, enjoying a piece of cake that your child made, playing in the yard with your dog in the fresh air, or simply for being healthy. It doesn't matter how big or how small; you have something in which to be grateful.

Happiness is a Choice

Humans have over 50,000 thoughts a day and 70-80% of those thoughts are said to be negative in nature. This is an incredibly sad statistic, but we don't have to be one of the individuals that make up the 70-80%. We have learned that we alone have the power and ability to control the thoughts that we focus on and control the thoughts that we act upon. Good thing, because it is difficult to take positive action and reach our life goals when we are unhappy and feeling bad about ourselves. Being unhappy and stuck in a negative place does not motivate or inspire us at all. The best news you may ever hear is that happiness is a choice. Yes, we can be happier and it is as simple as shifting into a more positive state of mind. Inspiring quotes, pictures, motivational music, remembrance of a happy event, or just about anything that gets a person energized, can be used to put us in that positive place in our mind. Things like quotes help to shift our thinking, allowing us to look inside ourselves. When we look inside, we find our passion, reconnect to our life direction, and get equipped to take action. Deliberately focusing on things that bring and keep us in a positive place is the key. Deliberate happiness can secure countless rewards, physical, mental and emotional, today and long into the future. We just need to make the effort.

Every day we can make the decision to pick a piece of happy fruit or dreadful fruit.

Genetics and life events can definitely affect our state of happiness, but only if we allow them. Our choices of what we will allow to reside in our minds is where we have control, and our choices can make a huge difference in our quality of life and overall happiness. Think about a yellow flower. Pause and see the yellow flower. Think about a blue ball. Pause and see the blue ball. Think about a red chair. Pause and see the red chair. Now pause and think of a happy thought. Pause and see this happy thought. Choosing happiness is as easy as seeing a yellow flower, a blue ball, or a red chair.

Choice is the Answer

Let us consider those that we deem successful. Successful people have higher self-esteem, are more self-aware, and are not afraid of change. They have a positive view about learning new things and believe that they can achieve their personal goals. These individuals take responsibility for their actions; they live by a set of positive values, and are persistent, not

It is better to take many small steps in the right direction than to make a great leap forward only to stumble backward." –Proverb

giving up when the tough times come knocking on their door. Successful people tend to attribute their success to their personal motivation and ability, not to luck or random chance. Most importantly, they tend to remember their successes and de-emphasize their failures. Why would any one of us want to emphasize our personal failures? Not sure, but many individuals do just that. Dwelling on personal failures will not make us happy. The true meaning of happiness is not the same for us all. As we decide what happiness means in our own lives, consider that happiness is a choice. We are the driver of our own life, and as we travel down the road, we always have choices about which direction to take when we reach a fork in the road. The people we pick up along the way can influence us, but we must remain in control of our life's direction. The choices we make are crucial to creating more joy in our lives. If we want a happy life, we need to create it!

Choices influence the path of our life. We want to decide what our lives will be. Our life belongs to us individually and we want and need to control the path as much as possible. Controlling our own destiny is empowering and un-limiting. Others are not likely to make the same choices that we would make for ourselves so why should we give our power to make choices and control our destiny to someone else?

Why do we choose chocolate or rainbow sprinkles? It's one thing to choose not to have sprinkles but something else when we make the distinction between chocolate or rainbow sprinkles. We all have a preference and maybe the answer isn't very mind blowing; I have always chosen chocolate sprinkles, I like to mix both because it tastes best that way, or I think rainbow sprinkles are fun. When we start thinking about the choices we make then we are more likely to adjust our choices if they are working for us. Dip your cone in whatever sprinkles bring you closer to Cinque!

Choice

ACTIVITY

Write a New Story

You are the author of your life story. If you aren't fully happy with your story as it currently reads, then write a new one. Your life story is the one that you recite, so recite a story that you will enjoy.

Old and New Story Example:

<u>Old Story</u>: I want to lose weight and have wanted to do so for 10 years. It started as a few pounds but now it is 25 pounds. It is hard for me and the thought of changing my diet and exercise routine is exhausting. It seems the more times I try, the more times I fail and end up gaining even more weight.

<u>New Story</u>: I want to remain healthy and get healthier each passing day. It is easy to make healthy food choices and move my body regularly because I know every small choice and step I take leads to me feeling revitalized and strong. I know if I eat more or move less then I can counter the effects easily.

Write your story here:

Old Story: _____

_____

_____

_____

_____

New Story: _____

_____

_____

_____

_____

We all have a story to tell. When we recite our story, how do we feel? If our personal story doesn't make us warm and fuzzy when we share it, then we need to stop telling it. Challenge ourselves to express a story that makes us feel inspired and positive; one that makes us happy.

Choice

FEEL THE THOUGHTS THAT MAKE YOU FEEL GOOD

How many of the thoughts we have each day are anxious, critical, defensive, or frustrated? Most of our everyday thinking is driven from the unconscious mind, which is by far stronger than the conscious mind. This is why it may feel like an impossible task to harness our thoughts. But like most things, a little practice can go a very long way. We must grasp onto the thoughts that make us feel good and that lead to choices that keep moving us toward our goals. Once we grab hold, we need to practice keeping them. For example, if a person has a bad day at work, then they should not repeat the story about the events that occurred. Repeating these events won't make them feel better. Rather, retelling the days events will only keep them swirling in a cycle of negativity. Reliving the negative conversations and events only serve to make these individuals more tense and unhappy. Instead, we should let them go and focus on the things that occur throughout our day that make us feel happy, joyful, accomplished, inspired, and accepted. These are the moments that matter most!

Humans are powerful creators of our own reality, yet many of us don't realize our full potential. Those people who are successful have learned to shine a sunbeam on what they really want in life and then create the belief to make that want materialize. When we believe it, we feel it deep in our very core. We do not have to live with the cards we have been dealt by life. If life has been tough, change its path and fight for a better life. It is worth fighting for! Get rid of those irrational beliefs that hold us back. Beliefs are only thoughts that we choose to keep thinking. No belief is set in stone. Unfortunately, humans have a great capacity for sticking to false beliefs. For example, humans once believed that the world was flat until someone showed us it isn't. This belief was shared for many, many years, until someone had the courage to step out, and challenge that way of thinking. What beliefs do we hold onto that are holding us back? If we really challenge those hindering beliefs, we will see them begin to crumble. As they crumble, there is opportunity to create new, more positive beliefs, and as we practice those new beliefs we will become stronger.

If you're a poker player then you know this is a lousy hand. First of all, you don't even have all the cards for Five Card Poker. A good hand can be built from anyone of these cards but this combination is a losing hand. Like in the song The Gambler states, "every hands a winner and every hands a loser" which means we can win or lose depending on how we play the game. You can discard those cards that you don't think will work for you. We want to discard the beliefs that aren't working for us anymore. The difference in life is that we know what's working and not working for us based off our current life feeling. We can ask ourselves how we're feeling and is it my desired Cinque. If not, then those beliefs are not working for us.

ACTIVITY

I'll Be Happy When...

When you ask yourself the following questions, consider some of the beliefs you have that you think are holding you back. Check the ones that apply to you.

I'll be happy when I…
- ___ have more money in the bank
- ___ lose weight
- ___ get promoted
- ___ retire
- ___ can buy _____
- ___ can slow down
- ___ can focus on myself
- ___ _____
- ___ _____

How many times have we overheard someone say, " I'll be happy when...?" Some people wait for *this* to happen or *that* to happen before they can feel happiness. Let's remember what happiness is. It is a feeling, an emotion. A feeling that is determined by our thoughts and we control our thoughts. The ability to be happy is just a simple thought away. A committment to choose happy thoughts over negatives ones. The committment to see the postive in situations versus the negative. A committment to creating a happy environment. What is committment? A committment is taking action and making a choice for the way we want to think and be.

It is sad to see others give up the control of their life's goals and direction, leaving it all up to chance. If we choose thoughts that make us feel happy, we can be happy right at this moment. By going to a happy place in our mind and remembering a person, place, thing or event when we felt joy, we are brought to our happy place and can relive this moment. We soon discover all the new, wonderful things that we are attracting into our life with this positive mindset.

Change Barriers

Many times we are our own worst enemy when it comes to making a positive change. We get stuck in our negative habits, and allow ourselves to be our own barrier. Most of the time we are not even aware that we are doing anything to sabotage our progress. Once we identify the sabotaging behavior, we can stop it and move forward.

> "The Chinese use two brush strokes to write the word 'crisis.' One brush stroke stands for danger; the other for opportunity. In a crisis, be aware of the danger--but recognize the opportunity."
>
> -John F. Kennedy

Gritty Lasagna: The Print in Blueprint

Negativity is one of the biggest factors that bar the majority of people from attaining personal growth. When we say things like, *can't, won't, don't* and use other negative words we keep reinforcing a negative mindset, which is why we should try to keeps these words out of our conversations. The key to successfully making core changes in our way of thinking is to replace them with positive words and encouraging thoughts. Being plagued by negative self-talk disease just continues to put barriers in our way.

As we make a commitment to remove these barriers, refrain from the following:

Excuses are the nails that build the house of failure." -Don Wilder

1. Stop complaining, period. Instead choose to view every annoyance, difficulty or unpleasant event as an opportunity to view the things for which you are thankful.

2. Excuses have no place in our desire for personal growth. It is most respectful when an individual can understand the importance of responsibility and be accountable for their actions. Trust in ourselves that we have the strength to obtain our goals, rather than make excuse after excuse to rationalize our behavior. If we want to take a major step forward in our personal growth, then we will stop making excuses today.

3. Take a moment and identify people in our lives that are toxic. Toxic people are quick to criticize and will make insensitive statements. By thriving on our inadequacies, these people love to point out our flaws. Toxic people prey on us when we are vulnerable and kick us when we are down. Why do we want people in our lives that take every opportunity to chip away at our self-esteem? Stay clear of these types of people. Toxic people are unhappy and insecure. They feel better about themselves when they are making others feel badly. Let's hold onto our own power instead of giving it away to others. We can choose to replace these toxic people with individuals who are supportive and want the best for us.

4. Don't play the blame game. Until we take total responsibility for every facet of our lives, our personal growth success will be restricted. Blaming anyone or anything in life might provide some temporary comfort, but ultimately it stunts our growth because it takes away our power. By blaming, we are giving everyone else the power to control our lives. This limits our dreams and keeps us from moving forward. Our past is the past. Keep it there. It has no place in the future.

5. Let go of the need to always be right. Many people cannot stand the thought of being wrong. Needing to always be right even at the risk of ending relationships or causing a great deal of stress and pain is destructive. It is just not worth it. Honestly, what does it matter who is right? Next time we find ourselves debating and arguing to convince someone that our point of view is correct; stop, take a deep breath and consider another person's point of view.

Choice

The path to our personal growth and our willingness to make the needed changes start by gaining control over the barriers that get in our way.

The "right side" of the bed doesn't lead to less stress. If you are tired, it doesn't matter where you lay.

Breaking Bread

A habit is something that is repeated over and over again. Habits can be the way we behave or the way we think. These habits can be positive or healthy benefiting us and assisting in our accomplishments or they can be negative or unhealthy habits that have an undesirable impact and prevent success in certain areas. Breaking unhealthy habit patterns is a choice needed to change the direction of our personal development since our personal actions determine the direction in which our life moves. The majority of our habits are unconscious, meaning they are automatic. If we are going to change our lives, changing the habits that do not provide benefit is needed. By activating the conscious thinking part of our brain, we can break the hold that an unhealthy habit has on our mind.

If you change nothing, nothing will change.

If you break the bread into small pieces before you begin to eat it, you won't choke on it.

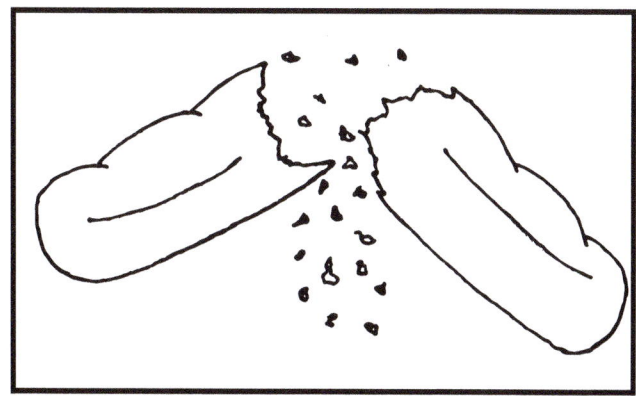

Habits are familiar and comfortable, and their part in our everyday life is effortless. Human nature is to keep doing whatever is comfortable and safe, which is resistant to change, and can be challenging for many people. Break the habit down into smaller, tangible actions to ensure we don't choke on it. Introducing something unfamiliar in order to break the pattern will cause some degree of discomfort. When we are uncomfortable, our discomfort can prevent us from allowing the change to occur and keep the adaption from taking root, even when we would like to make the change. It is important to stand strong and recognize that a choice to break this habit will have positive long-term effect. It is easy to say we must hang in there and persevere, but we must start where we are.

> Pull out your smart phone, go to a voice memo app, and create a positive self-talk recording. Every night before you go to sleep listen to the recording. Commit to doing this for three months and witness the major shift in your thought patterns and the ability to stop when negative self-talk creeps back in. No self-sabotage or self-limiting beliefs allowed. Use only healthy, positive words and thoughts to create a positive self-fulfilling prophecy.

ACTION BRINGS THINGS TO LIFE

Most people who say they have a strong desire to change a habit don't really want to stop the behavior, they just want to avoid the consequences and negative effects brought on by this target habit. It is great to say that we want to make modifications, but taking action is required. We cannot merely read this information and expect it will automatically create positive habits, expand our personal growth or help us reach our desired goals. We are required to do the desired work and stay on task. A great way to make sure we to stay on task is create an action plan. That sounds fine and dandy, how do we do this? Where do we start? We want to make a change and reach a goal, but feel stuck. We don't seem to be able to actually take action and start moving. With awareness we will know a problem exists, and we can take action to begin the problem solving process.

How can we be sure we are making the best decision possible…a decision that will lead us to success in reaching our desire goals? By asking a few simple questions before deciding what to do, we can be assured of making the best decisions possible. In addition, these strategies also help us avoid making impulsive decisions or not making any decisions at all. Remember, we always have OPTIONS.

OPTIONS

Process to making good decisions and making the best choice:

O   OPTIC-See the current situation
P   PREFERENCE-How do we want the situation to be now?
T   THINK-Think about how this situation will impact the future
I   INDENTIFY- Identify choice options
O   OUTCOMES-What are the possible outcomes to each choice?
N   NECESITATE-Commit to your choices
S   SELECT- Select a plan of action

Many life choices don't take into consideration the people who will be affected and impacted in the future. A responsible decision is one, in which, an individual considers others and their future before a decision is made. This may mean that they have to do a little research, like asking others what they think or looking for information about future possibilities. We do not have to do what others want; we just need to consider the implications and consequences of all the possible options. As long as we have considered the impact of our decision on others and our future, we are now free to choose whatever we wish. By thinking beyond ourselves and beyond the moment, we are more likely to select choices that have positive personal, social and future benefits. The choices we make today affect our lives tomorrow.

Immediate gratification contributes to the shortage in the number of responsible decisions made by some individuals. Acheivieving long term goals require gearing up for a marathon, not a sprint, because they result in delayed gratification. Sometimes our impatience for the arrival of a subsequent reward or the belief that there are no guarantees that there will even be a reward, stops us in our tracks. We would rather give up on our dreams and make choices that moves in the opposite direction of our dreams for an immediate satisfaction guarentee.

We are our choices, so choose wisely.

Gritty Lasagna: The Print in Blueprint

Scenario

Penelope

Penelope has a co-worker named Dana who is constantly pointing out Penelope's faults and the faults of those around her. One particular day, Penelope is over it. She is sick and tired of Dana's negativity and Penelope thinks about how she is going to handle the situation. She chooses to use the options process.

Dana

OPTIC
Penelope is angry because she feels like her co-worker, Dana, is constantly pointing out everyone's faults including Penelope's.

PREFERENCE
Penelope wants to feel calm at work and not be on the defensive and on the verge of exploding.

THINK
Penelope wants to be well-respected and viewed as a good leader so she can further her career and be promoted.

IDENTIFY
Penelope decides she has a few options.
1. She can choose to ignore the situation.
2. She can speak to Dana in a calm manner and explain to Dana that her comments are hurtful.
3. Penelope can tell Dana off, pointing out her own faults with the intention of putting her in her place.

OUTCOMES
Penelope considers each choice and the potential outcome for each one.
1. If Penelope ignores Dana, Penelope will continue to get upset and angry each time Dana does this action, and ultimately, she will go crazy over this situation.
2. If Penelope discusses things with Dana calmly, Penelope will have the opportunity to share her feelings with Dana in the hopes that Dana will understand how her comments have been affecting her co-workers and creating a negative office environment.
3. If Penelope gets into a confrontational conversation with Dana, pointing out her faults, Dana will get defensive. Dana will not be open to understanding Penelope's point of view, and will defend her actions, making Penelope feeling more frustrated. Both ladies will walk away feeling angry and nothing will be resolved.

NECESITATE
Penelope decides that her decision to deal with her current situation will be based on

her long-term professional goals and not what will feel good at the moment. Penelope decides she will write down exactly what she would like to say calmly to Dana. She will commit to keeping to her viewpoint and using "I" messages so Dana is more likely to hear what she is saying instead of getting defensive.

SELECT
Penelope decides she will casually ask Dana to come to her office on Tuesday morning at 10:00am. She will give herself 20 minutes to mentally prepare so that she can carry out her plan to calmly express herself. Penelope will read her notes while listening to soothing music and is sucking on a peppermint to keep her emotions in check, prior to Dana's arrival to her office.

In using OPTIONS, Penelope now knows she cannot ultimately control Dana's behavior. However, she is clear about her preferred feeling at work and how that will affect her future. This process has helped Penelope manage her emotions to get more of what she really wants in her life.

Use the OPTIONS process above each time you have a choice to make. Allow it to guide you to make the best of any situation to keep you on track to meeting your goals.

Action Plan

Awareness: If we don't know that a problem exists, how can we fix it? Without feedback from others telling us different, we believe that we are doing just fine. Occasionally soliciting feedback from our family, staff, friends, or colleagues is a good idea. Although, the fact that someone else has issues with our behavior does not necessarily mean that we agree. If someone suggests that our behavior is an issue, we must not automatically reject the possibility. Instead, we should try to understand how our actions might be affecting others, since it is not something that we have been able to see prior.

Motivation: Do we have the grit to persevere? We must put in the effort. Self-directing goal achievement is necessary. We have to want the change and be willing to do the work. So ask again, "do I have the grit to persevere?"

Identification: If we believe that we should make some changes, then it is time to identify exactly which behaviors we need to give focus and describe them in specific terms. If our goals are described in broad, fuzzy terms, break them down further and get more specific.

Substitution: Stopping behavior automatically implies that we will replace it with another. Any behavior change has a greater chance of success when we define it in positive terms instead of negative ones. If we want to eliminate a troublesome behavior, decide what helpful behavior to substitute in its place.

Habit Replacement: A successful behavior change means that new habits have been developed. Our current way of behaving is a habit, and we must change our behavior habit. It takes 21 days to change a habit. Ask yourself: do we have 21 days to devote to replace a negative habit with one that can lead to a lifetime of success?

Be Patient: Remember change is a process not an event. It will not happen overnight. Be aware that others may not immediately notice any change in our behavior. There is always a gap between the actual change in a behavior and the acknowledgement of that change in the perception of others.

Stay Committed: The path to reach our goals is rarely straight forward, and relapse is a real consideration. We cannot get down on ourselves when we mess up. Pick ourselves up by the bootstraps and start again. Learn something about ourselves with each relapse and recognize that these opportunities are helpful for successful change. Relapse is just another opportunity to learn and grow. Staying positive during this period of time is extremely important. Keeping that positive headset focuses our thinking in line with what we are trying to achieve.

Reward Yourself: To break a habit, it is helpful to reward ourselves for engaging in the substitute behavior. The reward can be anything we desire. We just need to choose a reward that will bring personal enjoyment and something that is truly wanted. Rewards will have the most impact if they are received soon after engaging in the substitute behavior.

GRIT It Out

Everyone goes through some level of crisis at some point in life. These hard times are true tests of our GRIT: Growth, Resilience, Integrity and Tenacity. Crisis management is about surviving a rough patch in life. How we react when we encounter a personal crisis is crucial to how we come out of it. Some people make the best out of these times and put themselves to test and come out victorious, with minimal damage and a drive to turn things around. Those who don't are the ones who find themselves spiraling out of control with a loss of what to do to manage.

Some individuals are able to weather crisis with GRIT, because they know it is an opportunity to be strengthened by the adversity rather than weakened. No matter what kind of crisis hits, we have far more control over our success and situational outcome than sometimes we believe. Believing we have choice not only gives us control when a life-altering crisis strikes, but it also provides support through mundane, day to day bumps we hit while going through life. A growing body of research shows that subjects who try to avoid upsetting feelings have far higher levels of post-traumatic stress disorder than those who experience and express their emotions. Knowing how to come through tough times stronger and healthier is all about knowing how to go UPHILL.

1. **U**nderstand
Crisis events are more common than we think and affect everyone. Find solace in the fact that we are not alone. Crisis events are just problems. Start off by identifying and understanding the problem. There is no sense in moving forward without understanding what the problem is and how it is affecting us. Accept the feeling without blame.

2. **P**lan
Time to Plan. Have a plan ready so that we can better solve a problem or a crisis when it comes along. Having a contingency plan and possibilities support our path for change. Design a pathway to tackle problems and stick to it. Stay aware of our surroundings and recognize when and where a crisis might occur. Planning is the single most important thing in personal crisis management. This allows us to side step the crisis before it begins.

3. **H**elp
Do not be afraid to ask for help and assistance from others. Asking for help is not a sign of weakness. Reaching out for help is a sign of strength. Even the best made plans can fall apart and it is helpful to have people available that you can call. Do not choose to face challenges alone. Four shoulders are always better than two.

4. **I**mplement
With a crisis management plan in mind, implement steps to tackle the situation causing the most issues. Start off with smaller things instead of trying to tackle the whole problem at one time. Take it one step at a time. Prioritize what needs to be done and sort the problems into small pieces. It is more manageable this way. Never try to attack an entire army at once. We will have much more success dealing with each individual soldier one at a time.

5. **L**earn
Now that we have tackled a problem, it is time to learn from the crisis situation. Think about what worked and see where the system broke down to come up with steps to avoid it in the future.

6. **L**ive
Live life without fear. We are now stronger, happier and on our way to change the direction of our future. Enjoy knowing we have control over situational events.

The next time we are faced with a difficult situation, try to remember to keep going UPHILL. No one is perfect, and some challenges will be harder to overcome than others, but lean forward and keep putting one foot in front of the other as we proceed up the hill. Once we get through the crisis, take some time to reflect on how we handled it, and how our actions affected the resolution of the situation. Celebrate the success and look forward to the next challenge, because now we know that we will be able to overcome it with confidence.

Even when we don't make a choice we are making a choice. When we are aware of our decision-making process and weigh the outcomes with what we really want, our path becomes clearer. Ultimately, we want the choices we make to guide us into the light instead of living in the dark. No matter what curve balls come our way, we can access the tools that will allow us to enjoy the things in our environment that bring us comfort and pleasure. That feeling grounds our daily practice and we know the homerun is coming.

Life Plan

Life Plan is the sidewalk to and from our house. The path that will lead us to places we want to go; the stepping-stones that will lead us to reaching our goals, obtaining our dreams, and achieving success.

Gritty Lasagna: The Print in Blueprint

LIFE PLAN

 *I was recently remembered of the 1979 remake of the movie **The Miracle Worker** (the one with Melissa Gilbert). I vividly remember that movie because, one, I was a huge **Little House on the Prairie** fan; two, it had a big impact on me and how I live my life. **The Miracle Worker** was about how Anne Sullivan, a teacher who worked with people who were deaf and blind, was hired to assist a young girl, Helen Keller, to communicate despite her disabilities. I wouldn't describe myself as someone who has an extraordinary memory; however, the details of that story have stayed with me for 35 years. I know I had an emotional connection to Anne and Helen's story; I like the way it made me feel. Helen Keller was able to overcome tremendous obstacles because she had an amazing teacher in Anne Sullivan who was compassionate and patient. That woman had grit! There are so many lessons to learn from each of them, but the reason I share the impression their story had on me was because it may have been one of the first stepping-stones laid down for my life plan. At 8 years old I wasn't creating a personal mission statement to create a self actualized life…keep in mind I was still at the age that the sound of the ice cream truck caused me to spontaneously jump over fences and sprint up the next street over to catch it; however, I did notice how The Miracle Worker made me feel and now had a great visual of a teacher overcoming adversity by not giving up on her student. In other words, notice how you feel, imitate an example or picture it in your mind, and decide what it is you actually want, really want, at the core of yourself. These are the beginning sparks of an excellent business, relationship, or personal life plan. I knew at 8 that I wanted to be like Anne, I don't need to be center stage, but I want to be a part of helping others strive to be their best. That's it…that's my mission!*

The only thing worse than being blind is having sight but no vision. – Helen Keller

A Life Worth Planning

It is time to get the most out of our lives. So let this be the first day of the rest of your life. To do this, it is necessary to have a life plan. Without a strategy, many of our dreams will only be dreams. A life plan is the mechanism that turns our goals and dreams into a reality by giving us the tools to get to our desired destination.

A life plan can be simple. So consider these things:

- We have identified our Cinque; so allow it to be a guiding force to our desired destination.
- Time to design a blueprint for achieving our goals, and we can begin by identifying the steps that we are willing to commit to do.

The number of dreams we have had identified for our lives could fill the Grand Canyon. This is very exciting, but it can also be a bit scary. Why? Identifying our dreams now brings to light the fact that we now have choices to make. Do

Life Plan

nothing and let the dream sit there and be nothing more than just a dream or figure out a way to make the dream come true which means venturing into areas unknown. Either choice can be very uncomfortable, but the hope is that our individual decision will be to embrace the unknown and forge ahead. All that is well and good, but a dream without a plan, is just that…a dream. That's not going to get us very far. A plan, a blueprint of sorts, of how to get where we want to go is required.

ACTIVITY

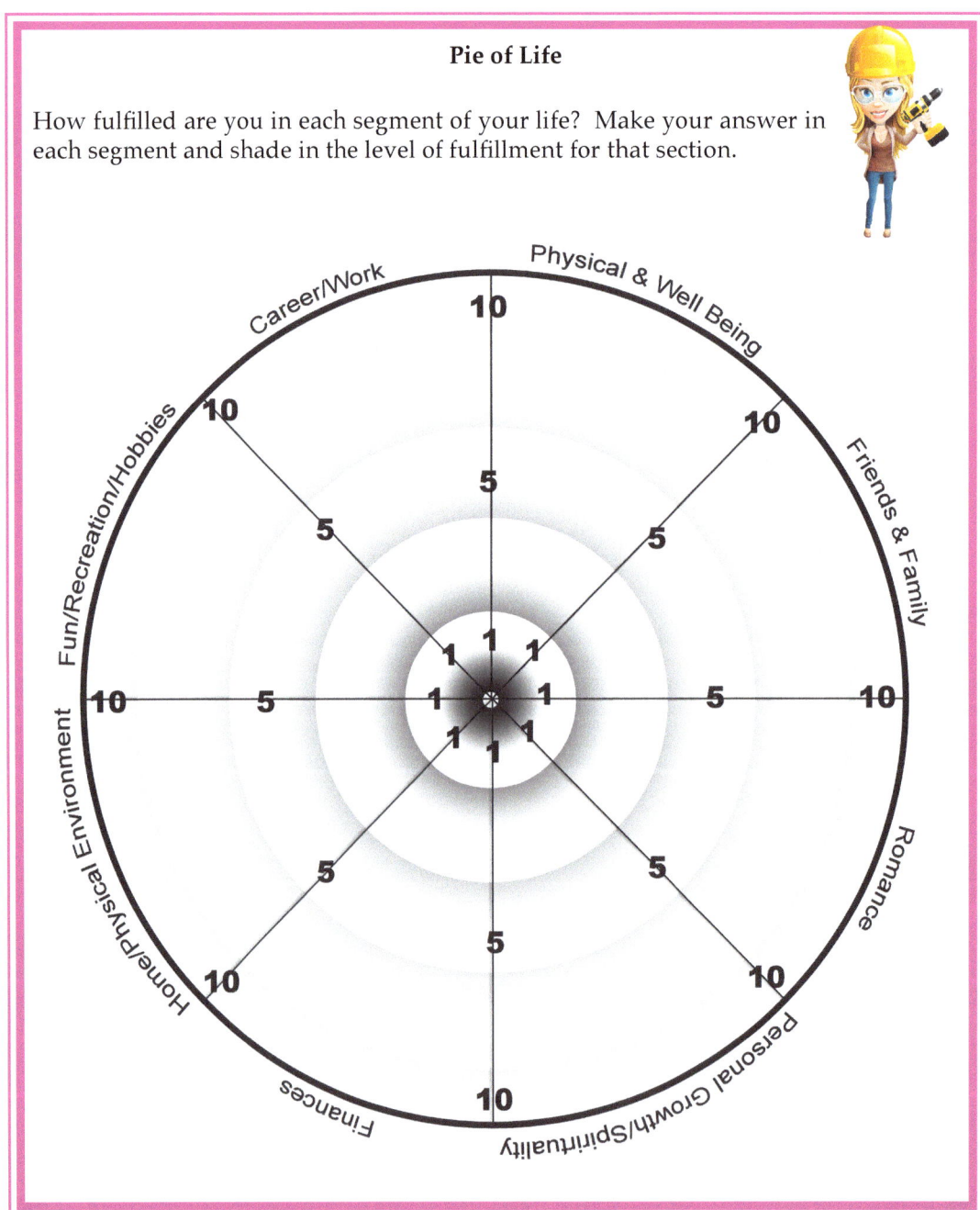

Pie of Life

How fulfilled are you in each segment of your life? Make your answer in each segment and shade in the level of fulfillment for that section.

Inspiration Creates Movement

Inspiration comes in many forms, which could be a simple quote or saying. Sometimes inspiration comes in forms of people and their stories. A succinct set of words can put things into perspective. A personal story such as Helen Keller's can help us reflect on our strengths instead of weaknesses. A bible verse, a passage out of a favorite book, an enduring tree, and an animal… the potential for inspiration is endless. We just have to look, listen, and most importantly feel for it. We may feel like we are vibrating under our skin; that's good Cinque and it's telling us to pay attention.

Now that we have identified what our Cinque feels like through the activities in this book we can use it as a monitor and driving force in our lives. Our Cinque gives us not only the feeling but also the vision we are seeking. Having a lack of connection between the feeling and a goal from beginning to end is what causes many people to give up on making goals. If we put the emphasis on our cinque then we will become successful because our feelings are guiding us rather than a finite goal alone. When I graduated college and had my first paid job as a social worker, I remember having two simple financial goals. My desire was to be able to pay for my car to be washed so I didn't have to spend the time doing it myself, and I just wanted to buy some shaving gel instead of using soap to shave my legs. It sounds silly, but there was more connected to those two simple goals then just a clean car and smooth legs. I connected those goals with the feeling that I was progressing from a college kid to an adult. It wasn't that I couldn't buy the car wash and the shaving gel, but I knew I wanted more than just reaching the goal. I desired that feeling…my Cinque! I still have moments in the car wash & lathering up my legs that I'm reminded to connect emotionally to whatever it is I think I want in this life.

Some people are really good at creating inspiration and can do this all internally. That's an excellent skill to have and it takes practice. If we don't have that skill yet we can create visuals to prompt us to get connected to our cinque. We can start by getting a piece of poster board and some old magazines, or you could create electronically and download an app.

The future belongs to those who believe in the reality of their dreams."

Got To Have Vision

A vision board is nothing new…people have been putting images in front of themselves for years to attain the things they want in life. Why do advertisers spend so much money on ad placement? Why do advertisers research the pivitol number of times an ad needs to be placed in front of potential customer s before those potential customers pay close enough attention to consider purchasing a particular product? The answer is…because it works!

Creating a vision board is like ordering from a catalog without considering the final bill. Go as big as would like just as long as when you look at it the thought is not: "that's never going to manifest in my lifetime!"

Here are some things to consider when putting a vision board together:
- Include words, phrases, verses that set the stage for a successful life
- Choose pictures or draw pictures that transport us to being in the moment
- Include things, people, and experiences that bring a feeling of excitement
- Develop a board to include all areas of our lives, and not just material things we want to acquire
- Keep it bright and colorful
- Think of the things we are grateful for and focus on our Cinque feelings
- Be specific; this should include what our heart most desires
- Personalize; combine pictures, words, phrases, quotes and make it personal
- Create in celebration of our self and make it a joyful task; put on music, invite friends over, enjoy your favorite dessert or beverage

Imagery is a very powerful tool! Thinking and believing in our desires and recognizing our goals are the place to start. Let the saying in the movie *Field of Dreams* guide us; "build it and they will come." We are in the beginning steps of executing the life we want when we design our blueprint.

Mission Possible

A personal mission statement is a great way to start developing our life plan. Consider the quality of life we desire; the overall feeling that will represent in our lives; the ideas that will be true to our passion. What is the overall feeling that is present when we think of having a high quality of life? That feeling should now be connected to every goal. When we are connected to our Cinque it can increase our self and social awareness. When we are more aware, we can manage our emotions more effectively and reach higher emotional intelligence. High emotional intelligence results in better decision-making skills and with more choices our stress level decreases. Less stress allows us to see situations more clearly and communicate with others in a more compassionate and effective manner. Effective communication skills improve our ability to develop long-lasting interpersonal relationships. The higher the quality of our relationships the more opportunities in the way of choices becomes available to us. A plethora of choices leads us to better planning and organizational skills. Designing a life plan is like starting a business and all businesses need to be lead with a clear, concise mission statement. Our life is the most important business we will ever run.

Break down our mission to an "I am" and "my purpose" statements. Once

What you think is what you are. What you pursue becomes your reality. –Babylon

we create these, a mission statement can be easily derived.

When we state what we want to believe about ourselves, as it's a present belief, for example, "I am a energetic, joyful, and giving person", it creates a clearer purpose, which may be "to feel good, enjoy life, and help others feel good and increase the quality of their lives". My mission is to create a joyful environment for myself that includes love and passion because that will make me feel energetic and alive. When I feel abundance, I want to share my joy and passion with others.

Print in Blueprint

As with any job, it is always easier when we have a plan. Our blueprint serves the same purpose. When we create this blueprint to address our individual needs and characteristics we are putting our personal touch on the plan, which will make executing the life plan easier and more enjoyable. To avoid creating a blueprint for a house that is never built, we need the correct tools. These tools make the job more efficient and cause less frustration as we do the job at hand. Identifying our blueprint will help get us started and using the appropriate tools to build our goals is essential. Anyone can say they are going to achieve a goal, but knowing how to turn it into a reality is an art form. Now is the time to take small steps and leave our colorful prints on the ground so we know the path to the home we want to live in.

Why do we need to PRAISE our goals? Consider this. Sunday night we are gung ho about our new exercise plan, but by Wednesday our lofty goal of exercising as soon as we get home from work has been blown off our radar. Sometimes we don't even realize we haven't taken the first step of the plan until days after our intended start date. Why do we do this? Do we not really want the goal, was it a terrible plan, or are we not capable of achieving a goal like this…what's the problem? There are so many questions we ask ourselves. Asking our self some questions is good. However, repeating the same thing over and over again and expecting a different result is the definition of insanity. Let's minimize our insanity and make a goal plan that will work with us and not against us. We want to ignore our plan because we know we are not even close to doing what we said we would do. To create the most effective plan to reach our goals, we must follow some simple guidelines. If it's too complicated then we won't do it. Keep it simple and PRAISE our goals!

P-Positive
R-Realistic
A-Applause
I-Individualized
S-Specified
E-Evaluative

Gritty Lasagna: The Print in Blueprint

P   Write a goal in positive terms. No negativity allowed. Always, always, always write the goal using positive terms, like "I will embrace", rather than I will stop." Also consider the outcome in positive terms. Instead of " I will stop yelling…." Instead state, " I will use positive statements…" and make requests in a calm volume and tone.

R   Make sure the goal or goals are obtainable and reasonable." I will reward my children all the time." Well, this is just ludicrous. What happens when we need to deal with a child's negative behavior? Is it reasonable to think that we will be able to always reward our child? Or select a goal that is not obtainable within our goals specified time period. We can't become a doctor in 2 years if we haven't finished college yet.

A   Identify rewards for meeting short-term and long-term goals. First applaud our hard work and these rewards can be an added incentive to stay on track. Noticing the progress we have made keeps us moving.

I   Make sure the goal or goals we are working toward is something we really want. We want to be excited about reaching it, so this will help to keep us on track. It is very difficult to achieve an insignificant goal to us, just because someone else wanted it for us.

S   Specify a time frame for reaching our goal and evaluate our progress consistently. Do not leave the time period open. We must create some urgency to giddy up and go. If our goal is very large and feels a bit overwhelming, we should break it down into small, short-term goals. These baby steps will keep us on course and allow us the opportunity to reach personal achievement.

E   Write my goal out in complete detail including a way to gauge and test its success. "I will make positive statements to my child 5 times each hour and will place a hash mark on my hourly calendar each time I do this." This statement is specific in terms of frequency and how progress is measured.

A goal without a plan is just a wish – Antoine de Saint-Exupery

Believe the life you want is possible.
Believe that you deserve it.
Now make your plan and go for it.

Life Plan

Gritty Lasagna: The Print in Blueprint

ACTIVITY

Write down your goals for each segment of your life.

Life Plan

Gritty Lasagna: The Print in Blueprint

ACTIVITY

Follow the 6 simple steps above to create a goal using the goal plan diagram.

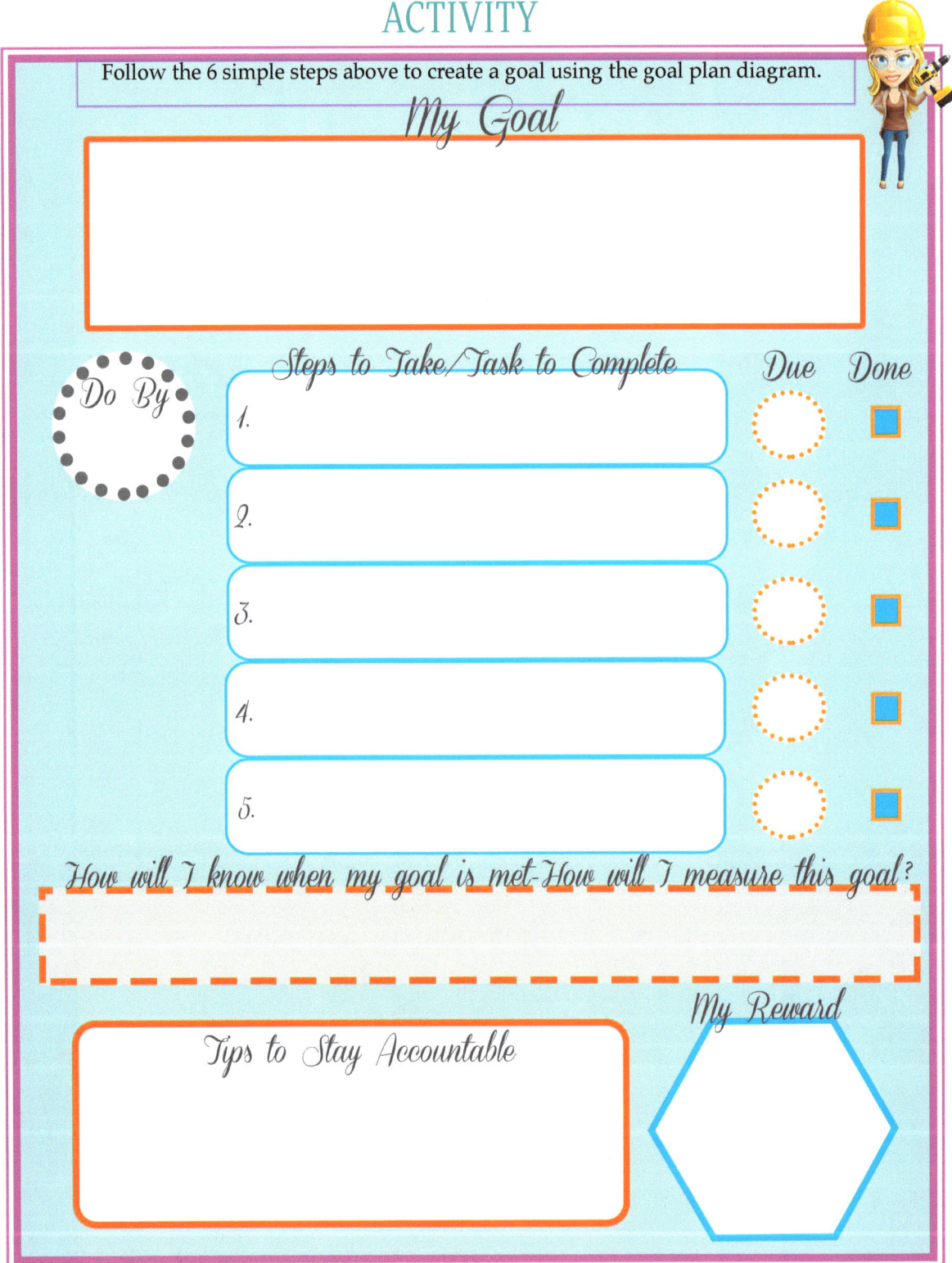

Life Plan

122

Extraordinary Capabalilities

Our world offers many extraordinary opportunities. Ever wistness the Salmon Run? It is one of the more astonishing feats in nature. It seems impossible, until we see it with our own eyes Unless an individual is an avid fisherman or an ichthyologist, the Salmon Run may be a foreign term. However, most of us have seen footage or a still shot of large salmon swimming and leaping upstream, and many times leaping into a bear's mouth. This natural event is called the Salmon Run and the salmon's purpose is not to leap tragically to their death; they are swimming upstream to return to their birthplace to spawn. It's not the spawning that is the extraordinary event; it's the actual path that the salmon take to complete their life cycles. Salmon are drawn to complete this life cycle by nature, but what if they weren't. Imagine how differently nature would be if animals made the choices that humans make; nay, I'm not going home to have babies…I'm quite enjoying my stay in the ocean. We have the ability to weigh our choices and consequences, and we have an opportunity to sit back and do nothing or create real meaning in our lives. When a salmon takes a leap upstream and is swept back down by the strong current it doesn't just give up. It tries again, and again, and again! It doesn't tell itself how stupid it is or complains that the water is too cold and that's why it didn't get a good leap. The salmon keeps moving to realize its life's purpose and isn't diverted from reaching its goal by appealing and enticing distractions that may come along. The salmon is going to stay on course despite setbacks. The Salmon Run is one example in nature of grit, and pretty much everything in nature has a gritty spirit. That spirit is what helps them survive and succeed.

People who innately have or learn this type of perseverance, the gritty ones, are the ones who will achieve the life they want. If we want to attain success on our path then we must get back up when circumstances knock us down. Mistakes and failures are a requirement; we are just trying to avoid the fatal ones. Everyone has moments of doubt, just don't marinate it in or with people who don't believe in our abilities. It's important to be aware of our current capabilities and then set realistic goals. Salmon prepare their bodies in the strong ocean currents for years before they engage in the Salmon Run. We want our state of mind in the preparation stage, which can be a long stage, to be connected to our Cinque because that will determine our ultimate success. You don't have to suffer through it: enjoy the process and be present in it.

You don't have to see the whole staircase, just take the first step." – Martin Luther King, Jr.

No Time Like The Present

We now have the tools to hammer down our goals that represent our overall life's plan. We have created the plan to achieve these goals, and we have identified the tools that can help us stay on track. It's time for us to start putting the plan in motion. It's time to make the commitment to live the life we desire. This is it; this is the time we have; just take a step. The attitude in Helen Keller's words will keep us moving, "I long to accomplish a great and noble task, but it is my chief duty to accomplish small tasks as if they were great and noble." Relish in the thought and emotions we will experience at the moment of fulfillment. Although goals will not be achieved overnight, just the process we will undertake will bring a sense of accomplishment to our lives and be a reminder to us of the big picture we are working towards. Living the life of our dreams is worth it. We are worth it!

Gritty Lasagna: The Print in Blueprint

MAKING FOOTPRINTS

Time to start making footprints, as we embark on our journey. Keep moving down the path we have mapped out. This book hopefully has helped you identify areas that are working well, and those that could use some adjustment. Use the Nexus Model and activities throughout this book as helpful tools to building a blueprint for success. As we plan for change, use the helpful techniques and sound concepts to strengthen our house where cracks may be visible, even if they are only visible to ourselves. This process becomes automatic as we stabilize our house and fill it with inspiiation. Ultimately we alone have the power, control and ability to achieve our life's desires, and when we create a positive mindset and follow our blueprint, we will stay empowered, and ultimately reach our heart's desire.

As we make our quest and work our life plan, we can use the following techniques to stay empowered:

1. Put focus on "self." This gives us the control to choose our own path.
2. Always come from a place of strength and positive-ness. Focus on what we can do well, and then do it.
3. Remember having weakness does not mean we our weak. It just means that there is a better way of doing things.
4. Take baby steps to stay on course without feeling discouraged.
5. Be mindful of maintaining positive thinking. Remember positive thinking leads to positive behaviors and feelings, which lead to positive results. Start with where we currently are, and build from there.
6. Embrace the concept of change. Change is required personal growth.
7. Start moving and find our grit. Commit to making the journey a successful one, remembering our current location on the path is not permanant.

If it doesn't challange you, it doesn't change you.

The Nexus Model is not a destination. It is an ongoing process that is to be incorporated into daily life. Embrace this concept as a personal guide and remember grit matters. The key to our "house" has always been in our back pocket. Just take it out, insert the key, and turn the knob. It's up to us to take the step and create our own print.

Social Awareness

BIBLIOGRAPHY

Cuddy, Amy. *Your Body Language Shapes Who You Are*. TEDTalks, June 2012.
Duckworth, Angela Lee, The Key To Success? Grit. TEDTalks, May 2013.
Jobs, Steve. *Standford Commencement Speech*. June 2005.
Tough, Paul. *Whatever It Takes*. Houghton Mifflin Harcourt, 2009.
Tough, Paul. *How Children Succeed*. Random House, June 2013.

www.ingramcontent.com/pod-product-compliance
Lightning Source LLC
Chambersburg PA
CBHW041553220426
43666CB00003B/52